WHEN SOMEONE

YOU LOVE  HAS

a

CHRONIC

ILLNESS

WHEN SOMEONE
YOU LOVE HAS
a
CHRONIC
ILLNESS

TAMARA MCCLINTOCK
GREENBERG, PsyD

PLAIN SIGHT PUBLISHING
AN IMPRINT OF CEDAR FORT, INC.
SPRINGVILLE, UTAH

ISBN 13: 978-1-59955-939-1

Published by Plain Sight Publishing, an imprint of Cedar Fort, Inc., 2373 W. 700 S., Springville, UT 84663
Distributed by Cedar Fort, Inc., www.cedarfort.com

LIBRARY OF CONGRESS CATALOGING-IN-PUBLICATION DATA

Greenberg, Tamara McClintock, author.
  When someone you love has a chronic illness : hope and help for those providing support / Tamara McClintock Greenberg, PsyD, MS.
    pages cm
  Includes bibliographical references.
  Hope and help for those impacted by illness in a loved one.
  ISBN 978-1-59955-939-1
  1. Chronically ill--Family relationships. 2. Caregivers. 3. Chronic diseases--Psychological aspects. 4. Chronic diseases--Nursing. I. Title.
  RC108.G76 2011
  616'.044--dc23
                          2011042378

Cover design by Angela D. Olsen
Cover design © 2012 by Lyle Mortimer
Edited and typeset by Kelley Konzak

10 9 8 7 6 5 4 3 2 1

For my patients and their loved ones

Other Books by Tamara McClintock Greenberg

Psychodynamic Perspectives on Aging and Illness
The Psychological Impact of Acute and Chronic Illness

CONTENTS

CONTENTS

ACKNOWLEDGMENTS

I am grateful to the wonderfully talented Elizabeth Bernstein, who helped to edit this book. Also, as always, I am especially appreciative of my husband, Andrew McClintock Greenberg, MD, PhD, for his thoughtful and perceptive ideas about how modern medicine has impacted both patients and loved ones, particularly when related to critical care situations. I am also thankful to Charles Spezzano, PhD. Charles is an incredible mentor in many ways, and he has encouraged me to bring psychological ideas to a wider audience. Additionally, I am grateful to Shersta Gatica from Cedar Fort as well as Kelley Konzak, my editor at Cedar Fort.

As with all of my writing, however, the patients I have seen over the last twenty years have provided the true support and inspiration for this book. I would not truly understand the ways that loved ones can help with chronic illness if it were not for those who have entrusted me with their thoughts, feelings, and ideas. Though there are many case examples used throughout this book, all cases are in composite form and do not represent any one individual with whom I have worked.

PREFACE

We are living in an unprecedented time in the worlds of medicine and longevity. Technology has changed the entire landscape of medicine and life in general. When many elderly people were born, life expectancy was around fifty-four years of age. Now, we all face a life span of much more than that, with recent statistics suggesting that the average life span is almost eighty years of age. Many of us will live even longer.

Illness will impact many of us as we age. If we are lucky and do not have to confront a serious illness ourselves, chances are someone close to us will.

This book is designed to help loved ones who know firsthand about the realities of chronic illness. Although there are many books designed to help patients cope with illness, there are relatively few offerings for those who care about someone who is ill and want to know how to help. This book will offer pragmatic strategies for loved ones and will probe deeper into what it means to cope with the challenges of chronic illness and to face the changes in close relationships that can result. Sickness does not occur in a vacuum. Particularly when illness impacts a parent or a spouse, illness occurs in the context of relationship dynamics and relationship histories. The tasks of coping are influenced by our own psychologies, the dynamics of patients, and what has transpired in the history of the relationship. I will discuss important ways that loved ones can become aware of and manage their own emotions so they can be better prepared to provide emotional support to the patient.

I will talk about the ways that helping too much can hurt, how to be mindful about the pitfalls of giving and caring too much, and the underlying motivations that might cause people to help more than they want to.

The topic of illness makes most of us feel anxious and helpless. This book addresses the feeling of helplessness in nearly every chapter. Understanding, tolerating, and coping with feelings of helplessness will help those impacted by illness better manage their own emotional life. When we feel helpless, we often don't know what to do or what to say. Chapter 2 will address the tricky and complicated terrain of words and provide specific advice on how to talk about chronic illness in the most positive and helpful ways. Subsequent chapters will address the pragmatics of how to get support when someone you love is ill and how to avoid seeking support in the wrong places.

We'll talk about other issues that make chronic illness complicated. You'll get concrete tips on how to work and communicate best with doctors, what to do when patients are not compliant, how to deal with denial (the patient's and your own), and how to handle issues related to pain.

Medical illness impacts everyone close to patients. Vicarious trauma and anticipatory grief are important concepts to know about and be prepared for, so we'll talk about those as well. Finally, I hope that loved ones of those with a chronic illness can feel empowered by reading this book. There are many ways to cope with illness successfully and many ways you can be aware of and manage your emotions that will have a real and positive impact on the person you care about who is ill.

How to Use This Book

Chronic illness affects people in multiple ways. Because of this, chapters in this book are wide ranging and designed to meet a variety of needs. For example, chapter 4 deals with how to manage denial in yourself or someone who is ill. This chapter is likely more geared toward those who are living with someone with illness. Chapter 2, "How to Talk About It," deals with struggles most people face when interacting with someone who is ill, whether they live with them, work with them, or know them in a social setting. Chapter 3, "Dealing with Doctors," provides a number of ideas for how all those involved can work with medical professionals in this increasingly complex landscape of medicine. Some of these ideas apply to loved ones who are acting as advocates, while others will be useful to everyone who encounters physicians and medical staff. Chapter 7 describes specific issues in helping someone cope with chronic pain, while chapter 8, "Avoiding Avoidance," addresses common fears you might face when considering how to engage with people who are ill.

You can read this book through from cover to cover or pick and choose what seems most useful based on your particular circumstance. Illnesses, as well as people, are incredibly unique and varied. Chapters in this book are meant to help you navigate the long and winding path when someone you love has a chronic illness, no matter where you are on the road.

GET READY FOR A LONGER LIFE

First, the good news: we are all living longer lives. Now, the bad news: we are all living longer lives.

Life expectancy has changed. Consider that the average life expectancy in 1920 was around fifty-four years of age. Today's life expectancy is between seventy-six and eighty years of age, though many of us can expect to live much longer. Already the number of people living well into their eighties and nineties is increasing, and chances are that many more of us will live to be centenarians. If we all could grow old in perfect health, aging would likely not be distressing. For many, however, illness is an unwelcome companion to aging. Taking into account the baby boomers, who represent the largest generation in history to age en masse, many more of us will confront illness than ever before.

Many diseases that used to end our lives no longer threaten us in the same way. For example, smallpox has been eradicated. We have vaccines for many diseases such as measles and polio. We have treatments for tuberculosis.

Breast cancer, which was once fatal, is now often referred to as a chronic illness. Previously, most people who had heart attacks died. This is no longer so. Though some do, many more people survive due to our advanced understanding of treatment and prevention. Doctors used to tell patients to stay in bed after a cardiac event, and we know now this is the worst thing people could do! Also, consider that aspirin has been shown in large-scale trials to be a major treatment and preventative medication for heart disease since only 1988.[1]

Modern medicine and medical treatments have come a long way in just the last few decades. People who are over seventy remember a time when all of the aforementioned diseases were fatal. Though the playing field of illness has been leveled somewhat, we now have new concerns. What does it mean that many of us live longer with chronic disease? Are we prepared? Do we even know what it means to be prepared? How do we help those we care about who become ill? Though many of us will struggle with minor or major illnesses of our own as we age, we will also likely see people close to us become ill. How can we help them and still take good care of ourselves? That is the purpose of this book. Loved ones trying to relate to and comfort those who are sick need their own tools for coping.

With the changes in the landscape of modern medicine, the nature of many illnesses has changed. One of the consequences of a long life is that those who become ill can stay that way for a very long time. Forty years ago, most people did not have to worry about chronic illness. Today, more than 133 million Americans, or 45 percent of the population, have at least one chronic condition, and 26 percent have multiple chronic conditions.[2] Chronic disease is the leading cause of death and disability in the United States.

Most of us are new to the terrain of chronic illness. Relatively and historically speaking, chronic and prolonged illness used to be a problem that affected few, not many. Heart disease, COPD (emphysema), arthritis, strokes, and Type II diabetes are all diseases that have changed the backdrop of illness. With the increase in lifespan, there is an increase in the number of and kinds of diseases that can plague us and those we love. In addition to the limitations these illnesses can cause, another new problem is that many more people struggle with chronic pain. All of these ailments reflect the good and the bad of modern medicine: many of us live longer, but many more live with chronic disease.

An unintended consequence of chronic illness is that many more of us serve in formal and informal caretaking roles. A recent AARP report notes that "in 2009, about 42.1 million family caregivers in the United States provided care to an adult with limitations in daily activities at any given point in time, and about 61.6 million provided care at some time during the year."[3] Increasing numbers of people who are ill will not only tax our economy and health care system, but also affect all of us emotionally.

Knowing what to say, what to do, and how to manage feelings when someone we love has a chronic illness is hard. Consider the following scenarios:

Your best friend of thirty years tells you she has been diagnosed with advanced cancer. She says she can't stop crying and can't imagine how she will manage chemotherapy.

Your husband of forty-eight years, who is now seventy, begins to act strangely. He uncharacteristically forgets to shower in the mornings, leaves his keys in the front door, and has started repeating himself. When you mention this to him, he tells you nothing is wrong.

You and your spouse have been having dinner with the same couple for years. Suddenly they disappear and are no longer available to meet. You contact the wife of the couple, and she tells you that her husband has just been diagnosed with multiple sclerosis.

Your mother, who has been living independently for most of her life, can't take care of herself anymore. She has been losing weight, forgetting to take her medications, and having trouble with walking and balance. You fear she will need to move into an assisted living facility.

Though all of these scenarios have varying degrees of emotional resonance, they contain a number of the same dilemmas. How do you manage your own anxiety about illness in general? How do you handle your nervousness about how to help or comfort those you care about who are ill? How do you deal with people who avoid you when they are ill? How do you articulate, as an observer, that you know something is wrong and want to help? And when someone does want to talk about the actual struggles of illness, like losing independence or fearing death, what do you say? How do you manage your own emotional discomfort? How do you communicate that you want to help; particularly when you are not sure that you can do anything to help?

In my work as a psychologist and psychotherapist over the last twenty years, I have explored these questions with spouses, children, extended family members, and friends of those beset by illness. There are no guidebooks for navigating this complicated emotional terrain. For many of us, the thought of illness is scary and leads to feelings of helplessness. When illness impacts someone we love, there are a number of uncertainties. This chapter and subsequent ones will address what to do logistically, strategically, and emotionally, as well as verbally, when someone you love is ill. Moreover, this book will help you identify and manage your own feelings when confronted with a number of dilemmas related to illness. You will learn the ways you can help or hamper the recovery of people who are ill, the ways illness in others forces us to confront our own vulnerability, how to really help those who are in physical pain, how to manage the demands of caretaking, and how to deal with denial—in yourself and in someone who is ill.

Illness reflects a level of vulnerability that is rarely a part of social interactions. However, as we all age, illness becomes more in the foreground than the background. Being prepared emotionally can allow us to feel more confident in talking with people who are ill, acknowledge the ways that we may or may not be helpful, and most importantly, cope with our own emotions. Additionally, as we will see, though we may feel at a loss when it comes to helping people we care about who are ill, managing our emotions can have a powerful effect on the ones we love.

Why Loved Ones Matter

It is striking that emotional reactions, such as grief and feelings of helplessness, in loved ones of patients get lost in the complex and fast-paced world of medicine in this country. Let's face it; doctors barely have time to attend to the needs of their patients, much less those of family members or friends. Emotional encounters in the arena of medicine (such as a physician asking, "How are you coping with this?") are still relatively uncommon. When this question is asked, it is far too often directed at the patient, while loved ones stand by silently. At home, family members feel uncomfortable talking about their distress, because they don't want to seem selfish or appear as if they do not care about the person who is ill. In friendships, such awkward feelings persist as well. Friends often complain that they do not know what to do or how to help. These feelings are understandable; in the face of the suffering of someone we care about, talking about ourselves risks removing the focus from the patient. On the other hand, when friends, partners, and family have a voice regarding their own emotions in response to a loved one's illness, they are more emotionally available to help. This availability is crucial, and not just for intuitive reasons. Managing emotions when dealing with illness helps not only us but the patients we care about as well.

Chronic illness is a family disease. By family, I mean to include all who are close to those who are ill. Partners, family members, and friends witness suffering and are all loved ones who experience illness vicariously. Their worry, helplessness, anger, guilt, and sadness often go unnoticed, and they feel alone with these emotions.

The lack of attention afforded to family members carries an ominous price. The psychological and physical health of caretakers suffer, with research showing that older adults who care for their seriously ill partners die sooner than people who are not caretakers.[4] Further, depression and anxiety are higher in family members (particularly those providing some aspects of caretaking) of patients with many kinds of illnesses, from dementia[5] to cancer.[6] Depression and anxiety are not just detrimental to psychological health; physical health is impacted as well, since depression and anxiety disorders serve as risk factors for several medical illnesses.[7]

And it's not just the health of family members that's at risk. When loved ones don't cope well, it affects the patient. Attitudes and behaviors of family members can influence how well patients take care of themselves.[8] When patients have positive and loving support, they are more likely to follow the advice of physicians. Additionally, stressful marriages and those that involve conflict can negatively impact health for reasons that are not well understood.[9] The importance of loved ones being able to manage emotions is not just intuitive; managing difficult feelings is crucial to both mental and physical health—for everyone involved.

Paying attention to yourself, as a partner, caregiver, friend, or watchful witness allows you to be more engaged with, and ultimately more helpful to, your loved one dealing with illness. It is not easy. But consider the work you do on your own emotional well-being to be an investment in your health and that of your loved one.

A growing body of psychological and medical literature, which will be described throughout this book, demonstrates not only that loved ones are as emotionally impacted by illness as patients, but also that when loved ones and patients think together about how to cope, it can enhance the support loved ones are able to provide. Staying engaged is important. For example, the ability of loved ones to support patients who are ill can erode over time and loved ones can simply wear down and not be as supportive as they want to be. When this happens, it is often related to the difficulties loved ones have giving themselves permission to take care of themselves.

How to Manage Anxiety When Confronted with Illness

There is a funny paradox related to sickness. If we are ill ourselves, many of us cope by finding ways to take control. But when illness happens to someone we love, we are limited in the kinds of control we have. Because of this, illness can be terrifying. The lack of control as it relates to illness is perhaps one of the most difficult challenges we will face. Illness reflects vulnerability, and in the face of vulnerability, many of us want to jump into action. But there is only so much we can do. In the early stages of illness, we are often relegated to waiting for news, diagnostic information, and plans for treatment. Waiting and not being able to do anything can be scary. Consider the case of Ken and his wife, Carol:

Ken noticed an unusual growth on his leg. He pointed this out to Carol, and she suggested that he immediately seek medical attention. Ken called his doctor's office, which gave him an appointment one month later. Carol was enraged. She felt that Ken was being lackadaisical in the face of what might be something serious. But Ken felt that Carol's concerns were exaggerated. Ken kept his appointment for a month later, though the couple argued continually regarding whether this was the right course of action.

Carol's anxiety was paramount, but Ken's wasn't. Although Ken was able to tolerate the stress of not knowing what was wrong with him, Carol was panicked. She did multiple Internet searches regarding what illnesses could possibly explain Ken's situation, and she became convinced that Ken had something serious and life threatening. She was consumed with worry about losing Ken. The couple engaged in near-constant arguing that ended up causing a rift in the relationship. When Ken finally did see a doctor and found out it was a benign growth, Carol felt embarrassed. Although Ken eventually understood this behavior as the result of Carol's love and concern, the couple endured a month of fighting that was unnecessary.

Anxiety is difficult to manage, especially when it comes to the ones we love. In illness (or questions of illness), as partners, friends, or family members, we need to tolerate uncertainty. Carol eventually understood that her anxiety stemmed from how much she feared losing Ken in general, and that resulted in behaviors she regretted.

Despite this good outcome for Carol and Ken, there are many instances in which a friend, family member, or loved one must endure actual illness. In these cases it is also hard to know how to behave. Consider the situation of Ashley:

Ashley's mother had been in renal failure for the past three years. Though she was on dialysis, her health had started to fail. Ashley lived a short plane ride from her parents, but given her work schedule, she could not go home as often as she would have wished. As her mother's health started to deteriorate, Ashley felt increasingly guilty. When she called her parents and asked if she should come home for the weekend, they often said no, that they could manage without her. This left Ashley in a terrible bind. Should she demand to go home to see her parents? Or should she stay where she was and focus on work? Although this decision would be difficult for anyone, Ashley developed extreme anxiety, which kept her from functioning at work. She constantly worried about her mother, lost weight, and was unable to sleep at night.

Ashley's situation illustrates the extreme distress that is common among people who are concerned about an ill loved one but who are not immediately available to help. Though Ashley's parents seemed earnest in their advice for Ashley to continue to work until her mother's health worsened, Ashley's anxiety and helplessness impacted her ability to function. In such situations, it is hard to know what to do. And though any of us would feel anxious in similar circumstances, it's important to remember that our suffering does not help alleviate the actual suffering of the one we love.

Illness makes most of us incredibly anxious. This anxiety is obvious in some ways because we worry about losing people we care about. Illness also reminds us of our own vulnerability, and many people can feel stressed—tortured, even—by worries about their health and vulnerability to illness. Further, when someone we love is ill, our experience of their illness takes place within the context of our relationship with them. When relationships have been conflicted or unsatisfying, it can intensify the anxiety we feel when people become sick. In subsequent chapters I will discuss many facets of how our relationships with others impact how we cope with their illnesses. As a starting point, however, it is important that loved ones become aware of and manage their own anxiety.

Techniques

Consider the following suggestions as a Band-Aid for dealing with anxiety in the short term. Getting control of the initial emotional discomfort we experience when someone we love is ill is often a needed first step so that we can think about other feelings.

Breathing Exercise

One of the best behavioral treatments for anxiety is a simple breathing technique, which can help to calm down our bodies in the face of stress.

Focus on your breathing. Notice if your breathing becomes shallow when you are nervous. This is common. Compare this to how you take deeper breaths when you are relaxed. Shallow breathing is a normal symptom of anxiety and is related to the fight or flight response, which will be discussed more in chapter 7. Slowing our breathing down when we are nervous allows us to take control of the physical effects of anxiety. It is like a natural drug that tells our bodies we are safe. Use this diaphragmatic technique to slow breathing when you are anxious:

- Place one hand on your chest and the other on your abdomen. When you take a deep breath in, the hand on the abdomen should rise higher than the one on the chest. This ensures that the diaphragm is pulling air into the bases of the lungs.
- After exhaling through the mouth, take a slow, deep breath in through your nose, imagining that you are sucking in all the air in the room, and hold it for a count of seven (or as long as you are able, not exceeding seven).
- Slowly exhale through your mouth for a count of eight, or as long as you can. When all the air is released with relaxation, gently contract your abdominal muscles to completely evacuate the remaining air from the lungs. It is important to remember that we deepen

respirations not by inhaling more air but through completely exhaling it.
- Repeat the cycle four more times for a total of five deep breaths and try to breathe at a rate of one breath every ten seconds.

It is important to practice this technique a few times a day, even when you are not anxious. The idea is to get your body and mind to recognize the difference between anxious and relaxed states. Additionally, practicing any relaxation technique, including diaphragmatic breathing, when you are relaxed allows you to develop and hone the skill of relaxing yourself. Being able to master this skill is important because you can then use it when you really need it.

Managing Worry

When we are anxious, our minds can kick into overdrive and we try to solve problems that cannot immediately be solved. Many people refer to an anxious mind as a rat on a wheel going nowhere. We may lie in bed contemplating how we could have handled a situation differently or imagining what we can do to help someone we care about. The problem with an overactive mind is that we can rarely act to make things better. For example, if you are lying in bed at 2:00 a.m. on a Sunday morning, there is likely little you can do to solve the problems you are worried about.

One way to soothe your mind in such a situation is to get out of bed and make a list of what you are worried about. Divide the list into two columns. One list should include actions you can take at a later time to solve a problem. Consider when you can take the action. For example, if you want to call your mother's physician, write down when you will do so. The other column should be worries that you can't take any action about. For example, you might write, "I am worried that my friend's cancer will come back." The goals of this exercise are to focus on what you can actually control and to place your worries outside of yourself as a way to postpone your worry. Tell yourself you will have plenty of time to worry later. Indeed, this is the great thing about worries: we can always come back to them! When we are worried, it is helpful to focus our energy on what we can actually do to take control and to tell ourselves that although we may not be able to do anything at the moment, we will try to take action when we can.

Life, Interrupted: When Illness Takes Over

Most of us take for granted the idea of good health. This is as it should be. Those of us who are born healthy and experience the health of those around us naturally expect that those we love will go on living healthy lives. Unfortunately, this is not always the case, and when someone we love gets diagnosed with a serious illness, it can be quite destabilizing. It can alter life as we know it. It can threaten the future of relationships as the vision of normal life quickly fades away. Things that other people take for granted, such as Saturday morning errands or a quiet Sunday brunch with family, are disrupted by the limitations of illness. Though life might have been hectic beforehand, when a loved one is diagnosed with an illness, it can change your entire worldview. And whether you are a partner, family member, or close friend, when someone we love is ill, normal life changes into a series of questions: "What will the future hold? Will we be able to exist as we did before? Will I be able to help my loved one deal with the terrifying uncertainty of this illness? And if I am alone to deal with all of this, how will I manage?"

Illness interrupts life. It changes everything that we come to expect from those we love. Such changes are disorienting. And since the person we love is the patient, we have to figure out how to help them and manage a plethora of disjointed feelings.

Although anxiety can be distressing, it can also help us. It can help us to mobilize our coping defenses. When we are trying to help someone we love with an illness, we can use it to harness the energy to fight, to encourage our loved one to fight, and to help find the right medical clinicians who can advocate on our loved one's behalf. But anxiety can also be paralyzing when we feel so overwhelmed that we stop functioning and don't know what to do. In the cases of Ashley and of Ken and Carol, we saw striking examples of well-meaning people who felt powerless in the face of a possible illness. They tried to manage their anxiety by being controlling or irritable, both of which served to make them even more helpless in terms of how they might cope. Though illness, or the threat of it, in someone we love can make us terrified, managing these feelings and anxieties allows us to maintain important relationships and helps us to help the ones we love.

The rest of this book addresses a variety of complex emotions as well as practical concerns that often impact people who are trying to help someone who is ill. Coping with anxiety is an important first step. However, even if you can't figure out how to control your anxiety about illness, just knowing you are anxious is important. Many people I have seen throughout my career have been anxious but have not realized it. Being aware of and mindful about anxiety is crucial. In this tenuous time of a long life, many of us try to ward off feelings that make us uncomfortable. However, some level of anxiety about our long lives and related uncertainties seems to be the "new normal" of living in the twenty-first century. Fortunately, we can all learn how to manage anxiety and deal with what we are afraid of.

CHAPTER 1
COPING CHECKLIST

- We are experiencing an unprecedented time of aging and longevity. If you find yourself nervous about the future, know that you are not alone.
- When dealing with uncertainty about illness, trust that a patient can decide how urgently to seek medical attention.
- Manage anxiety through the diaphragmatic breathing technique described in this chapter. Only you can control your own anxiety.
- Deal with worry by writing down your concerns. Distinguish what you can and cannot control. Tell yourself it is okay to postpone your worrying and that you can come back to it later.

Notes

1. P. Elwood, "The first randomized trial of aspirin for heart attack and the advent of systematic overviews of trials," *Journal of the Royal Society of Medicine* 99, no. 11 (2006): 586–88.
2. Centers for Disease Control and Prevention. Accessed May 1, 2011, http://www.cdc.gov/chronicdisease/overview/index.htm.
3. L. Feinberg, S.C. Reinhard, A. Houser, and R. Choula, "Valuing the Invaluable: 2011 Update The Growing Contributions and Costs of Family Caregiving," *AARP Public Policy Institute*, 2011. Accessed September 1, 2011, http://assets.aarp.org/rgcenter/ppi/ltc/i51-caregiving.pdf.
4. N.A. Christakis, and P.D. Allison, "Mortality after the hospitalization of a spouse," *New England Journal of Medicine* 354 (2006): 719–30.
5. M.L. Gilhooly, H.N. Sweeting, J.E. Whittick, and K. McKee, "Family care of the dementing elderly," *International Review of Psychiatry* 6 (1994): 29–40.

6. U. Stenberg, C.M. Ruland, and C. Miakowski, "Review of the literature on the effects of caring for a patient with cancer," *Psycho-oncology* 19 (2010): 1013–25.

7. C.J. Holahan, S.A. Pahl, R.C. Cronkite, C.K. Holahan, R.J. North, and R.H. Moos, "Depression and vulnerability to incident physical illness across 10 years," *Journal of Affective Disorders* 123 (2010): 222–29; M.C. Härter, K.P. Conway, and K.R. Merikangas, "Associations between anxiety and physical illness," *European Archives of Psychiatry and Clinical Neuroscience* 253, no. 6 (2003): 313–20.

8. M.R. DiMatteo, "Social support and patient adherence to medical treatment: A meta-analysis," *Health Psychology* 23, no. 2 (2004): 207–18.

9. J.K. Kiecolt-Glaser and T.L. Newton, "Marriage and health: His and hers," *Psychological Bulletin* 127, no. 4 (2001): 472–503.

chapter two

HOW TO TALK ABOUT IT

Illness makes us uncomfortable. No matter how sensitive we are, no matter how well we listen to others, and no matter how much illness has touched our lives, bodily limitations remind us of our vulnerability. When people we care about suffer, it can make us feel helpless. We are unable to take away their worry, their physical pain, and the suffering they must endure.

It also goes without saying that illness reminds us of death. Death is not something most of us like to think about. Ernest Becker's 1973 Pulitzer Prize–winning book, *The Denial of Death*, points out that one way we deny death is to focus on the desire to be a hero. Being a hero, in this context, refers not only to our own basic need to feel powerful and the biological desire to preserve ourselves, but also to the power to cheat death. Ancient ideas of heroes support this argument: "The hero was the man who could go into the spirit world, the world of the dead, and return alive."[1] Surviving death was the link to power.

Becker goes on to argue that one way some of us deny death is to focus on success, gratification, love, sex, money, and all the things that make us feel powerful and in control. These things, such as the need for love or the need to make money to survive, can serve as distractions, while simultaneously increasing our sense of self-worth. It is as if we are saying to ourselves, "Only the weak can die. If I can be powerful, then I can live forever." Though many of us spend a lot of time trying to develop power and control, we still get reminded of our limitations. People we love die. Friends and relatives become sick, and we cannot save them. Death also symbolizes our own limits in general. It shows us that our accomplishments and achievements are temporary. Though we might achieve success in this lifetime, the painful reality is that there is a shelf life to our productivity. No matter what we possess, nothing is permanent. Understandably, this makes us quite anxious.

Against this serious philosophical backdrop, it might seem trivial to focus on how to talk about illness. But words matter. What we say to people we care about has a lasting impact. People remember what loved ones say when the chips are down. For example, a patient newly diagnosed with a severe illness told me that one of her friends made the comment, "Oh, I thought I would die first." My patient did not communicate anything else about this interaction, such as eye contact, tone of voice, or even the emotional manner in which the comment was delivered; rather, she simply told me the words that were spoken. It was obvious the profound effect her friend had in failing to be empathic.

Many people worry about saying the right thing. They don't want their anxiety to get in the way of being supportive. Putting some thought into what to say, how to say it, and what to do when someone is ill is a worthwhile investment. Perhaps part of the anxiety in knowing what to say has to do with our desire to be a hero to those we care about. Being a true hero is a tall order. Being a thoughtful, caring witness and loved one, however, is something that we can all achieve. It just requires a little thought and reflection.

So, What Do You Say?

When someone is sick, it is customary to ask for a brief update and then change the subject to something lighter. When people let down their guard enough to acknowledge that they aren't quite sure how to help someone who has been affected by illness, the first thing they say is, "I just don't know what to say." This is a good starting point because it confronts the fact that there is often no right thing to say or do. Being present, aware, and mindful is what matters most. That being said, there are some things that can be construed as not helpful, and I'd like to help you avoid those things. In other words, if I had put it in one sentence, I would say, *be present and try not to say offensive things.*

If we can manage our anxiety about illness, this can be easier. There is no seamless way to talk about illness. Awkward moments are normal, but patients can usually tell when someone is simply anxious and awkward, versus someone whose anxiety spills out of them in a way that disregards the feelings of the patient. One of the main goals is to convey that what you are saying really stems from an attempt to help the person you care about and not from trying to get rid of some bad feeling within yourself. For example, the woman who said to my patient that she thought that she would die first was probably trying to be supportive. She simply got so anxious that an insensitive comment slipped out in a confusing attempt to help herself as well as my patient. I doubt this woman was trying to be hostile or insensitive; it just seemed that way. Anxiety makes us all say things that we don't quite mean, but people can be very perceptive. If a person makes a comment to help himself or herself feel better, patients perceive this.

Recently, the husband of a casual acquaintance died suddenly, and I found myself making excuses to avoid the phone call I knew I needed to make. Though my procrastination lasted less than a day, I found myself wondering what I could possibly say to help. This is often the reason that people avoid friends who have been affected by illness. Sadly, worrying about saying the right thing can be more about our own egos! "Will I be helpful enough? Will I say the wrong thing? How can I make this better?" These are all questions we ask ourselves. Avoidance is the wrong approach. People affected by illness or loss need to know you are there. And when someone is grieving or ill, they tend to understand that people may not have the best set of social skills. The important thing is to make contact and let them know that you are thinking of them. If you can, offer to help. But if you offer, make sure you mean it, because some people will take you up on it.

Another important point is to avoid platitudes and superficial statements that try to make sense of an event that often is nonsensical. The number one complaint I have heard from many people over the years is how distressing it can be when someone says, "Everything happens for a reason." Though it might be the case that your friend has strong religious beliefs that could be a source of solace, such as a belief that God or a higher power may be watching over a patient, people are usually pretty clear regarding whether they want religious advice. Addressing emotions and avoiding attempts at explanation is often more helpful, at least initially. Statements like, "I am sure you are going to be a stronger person from this" run the risk of negating the actual suffering of the person you care about. Though it may be true that adverse events can be opportunities for growth, it is better to try to match what someone is feeling in the moment. Statements like, "I am so sorry. This is horrible" are often perceived as more genuine, particularly during the early phases of illness. You can then wait for cues from the other person in terms of how much he or she wants to get into a conversation about what has happened, including spiritual beliefs, which may be soothing to talk about.

Another common complaint I have heard over the years from patients has to do with how the appearance of illness can be confusing to people. Many well-intentioned people say to someone who has a chronic illness or chronic pain, "You don't look sick." Unfortunately, this comment falls squarely in the "Offensive Things" category. Many people who are ill do not appear to be. I think the temptation to make such a comment is not due to malevolent intent, but because many of us grew up identifying people who were ill by obvious signs: a loss of hair from chemotherapy or a wheelchair. We learned to identify people who were sick in a particular way that no longer applies. The fact that many people who are ill or in pain don't show it is likely an example of how the landscape of medicine has changed. For many of today's observers, illness is not obvious, and we have to tolerate some degree of ambiguity, not knowing who may be ill. The advice I usually give to loved ones in such situations is that if someone says they are sick or in pain, take them seriously. Many illnesses, especially today, are invisible to the casual observer.

Ask Questions

When an old friend of mine developed a rare illness, we talked about dying, what she thought might happen after death, and how her religion played a role in her thinking. We also talked about practical things: what medications she was on, which doctors she was seeing, and how she managed work in spite of her fatigue. The main thing is to be available and to talk about whatever the patient wants to discuss. I always say that we should let the person who is ill decide how the conversation will evolve. Perhaps because I am a therapist, I am an advocate of asking questions. Questions, when communicated with genuine interest and concern, are very calming to medical patients, who often appreciate the chance to talk about the details of treatment. There is no stupid question when it comes to medical treatments and illness. In many cases, asking questions is the safest way to communicate interest. If people do not want to answer your questions, they can simply change the subject. When this happens, I take it as my cue to back off.

One question that we should avoid is related to prognosis. We may wonder what someone is hearing from doctors regarding the projected course of illness; in general, it is better to wait for the patient to bring it up. For some people, not thinking about prognosis is a crucial coping strategy. Some people may also deny what they may have heard from physicians if the news has been bad. Regarding this kind of denial, I often find it is better to give people space.

It is also important to say that I don't take it personally when people don't want to answer a question. I am attempting to indicate interest, but I don't want to be intrusive. So if someone does not answer my question, I just read this as a sign that my friend or family member may feel overwhelmed. Achieve a balance by letting your friend know you care but having the conversation on their terms.

Be Flexible

I know it might seem as though there is no way to get it just right. But "just right" has to do with being sensitive to what others need, backing off if people don't want to get into something, and communicating openness. If someone does not want to talk about something in one situation, it does not mean that they will not want to tomorrow. Patients need to know that loved ones will be there when they need them. Because of the traumatic nature of illness, many people need to feel as if they are in control of how and when they talk about their illness experience. As loved ones, it is really not that hard to let someone who is ill decide when they need us. We just have to be flexible.

Being flexible requires us to manage our own anxiety and fears of illness. As discussed in chapter 1, this can be hard to do. If you are with someone who is ill and you find yourself anxious in a way that might make it hard for you to be empathic, don't worry. We often have many opportunities to get things right with people we care about. If you are anxious, don't try to cover it up. One of the things that patients often find difficult is when someone is offering help but in an overcontrolled way. You may be wondering what I mean by this. Overcontrolled is when people try to help but their anxiety is so close to the surface, it threatens to overwhelm. People who are controlling their emotions can seem "off" when talking about illness. Their words may be benign, but they are expressed in a monotone voice or in a restrained way. Being and appearing overly rigid when trying to express emotions or support can seem odd or awkward. I have a friend who does this. When I say something that makes her nervous, she offers support, but it often feels false or hollow. She might make a brief comment such as "Oh, boy" and then say nothing else. In other words, she gets too caught up in the worry of what to say, and what she does say feels false to me. A better strategy in such situations is to acknowledge how you are really feeling, combined with the message that you want to offer more than you are able to. For example, you might say, "I want to offer something to you right now, but I am feeling overwhelmed and worried that I won't know what to say or even how to be helpful." Comments such as these go a long way in communicating how much you care. What matters most to patients is that they have some sense that you are trying to be helpful. But we cannot always be. I have been in situations in which I have had to say, "I don't know what to say or how to help. I feel helpless." I have never had anyone get mad at me for such comments, as this is often a real expression of how sad and helpless I feel, but how I wish I could compose myself better to say something more useful. Ironically, such statements are often very well received because I am expressing how much I want to help but also acknowledging the limitations of what I can really say (or do) to make things better. In other words, the interaction is about them, not about me. We are not on stage when trying to help someone who is ill.

Extending the acting metaphor, we as loved ones are not the main characters. We are simply in supporting roles trying to help the person we care about. As supporting actors, we can offer a lot; even when we feel helpless, we can communicate how much we care.

We can also offer to do things for people. It is useful, when asking if there is anything you can do, to make specific suggestions. For example, "Would you like me to go with you to your next doctor appointment?" and "Can I cook some food and bring it over?" and "Can I help with your laundry?" are great things to say to friends who are facing illness.

Regarding those who are closer to us, it is okay to offer help but also to feel comfortable in setting limits on what you are able to do. One young woman whose father was dying of cancer provided a remarkable example of limits. She went home as often as she felt she could, and she restored herself in between visits at home by seeing her boyfriend. She told her mother that she wanted to help and would continue to help but that she had to keep working and living her life in order to keep her sanity. Though she canceled trips that she did not feel were necessary, she also kept doing the things that she needed to do to maintain her identity. This woman demonstrated remarkable clarity and maturity. Although we may want to help, if we don't take care of ourselves, we have little to offer. Our own self-care and our own self-awareness make us much more adept when we need to care for people who are ill.

Don't Try to Cheer People Up

Sometimes people affected by illness don't want to talk about it. That's okay too. People with illness often relish the breaks they have when they do not feel like a sick person. They look for friends and family members who can treat them as "normal" people again. This does not mean that patients will necessarily act happy. In fact, it can be quite distressing to medical patients when they feel that people are trying to get them to feel or act in a good mood.

When we try to cheer people up who are ill, it can be more about managing our own anxiety than about really trying to help. Avoid trying to make people happy. People who are sick are often unhappy, and it is not our job to change that. When we try to cheer people up, it can communicate the message that we do not want to hear about what they are going through. Forcing happiness can feel false. Though patients often feel they have to put up a front when they are with doctors and certain loved ones, don't make them feel as though they have to pretend in front of you. Be present. Ask questions. And if it is too much for you, say so and don't pretend. Pretending leaves patients feeling alone and worse than they did before.

It's Okay to Be Anxious

Thinking and talking about illness makes most of us anxious. If you try too hard to deny your own anxiety, it makes it hard to be present for those you love. By acknowledging anxiety and not being critical of yourself, you can be more present and less worried about what you say. Though many of us fret about saying the right thing, trying too hard to pretend that illness doesn't make you anxious can result in insensitive comments coming out.

Most of us would choose not to talk about illness. Denying death and vulnerability is common, particularly in US culture. In many ways, this denial is what allows us to function day to day without being depressed. When someone becomes sick, it reminds us of what we often try to forget: our bodies fail us and life is finite. In order to talk about illness, we have to pull ourselves out of denial and into the present.

CHAPTER 2
COPING CHECKLIST

- Be aware of the boundary between your own anxiety and the anxiety of the person you are worried about. Be aware of whether you are saying something to make yourself feel better or to provide comfort.
- If you don't have anything to say, it is okay to just be present.
- Don't try to cheer people up and don't force them to be happy. This may not be what they need.
- Don't talk about a poor prognosis unless the other person engages you in this discussion. Follow that person's lead in conversations.
- Don't worry about questions or censor genuine curiosity. There are no stupid questions. Something that might seem trivial is important.
- Don't be overcontrolled. Talk when it feels genuine. If you don't have anything to say or you feel helpless, simply state how you feel.

Note

1. E. Becker, *The Denial of Death*. (New York: The Free Press, 1973), 12.

chapter three

DEALING WITH DOCTORS: WHAT EVERYONE NEEDS TO KNOW

Medicine is not what it used to be. Doctors are more pressured and have less time for patients than ever before. Although lack of time is a major complaint among people I see who need doctors, another common concern I hear from my patients is the disquieting absence of bedside manner. Although some physicians are great at offering emotional support to patients and loved ones, I always tell people that in order to manage illness successfully, they must adapt to the culture of medicine. By "culture" I mean the attitudes of medical professionals and the hurried nature of appointments, which can seem manic to those not familiar with the world of medicine. Doctors and medical staff often seem to move, talk, and think fast. Dealing with medical professionals can feel a bit like entering a foreign country, one where there is not room for emotions or reflective thought.

This chapter will serve as your guide to dealing with doctors. There are a number of unspoken rules of behavior in medicine, as there are in any culture. Knowing these rules can go a long way in making sure that you and the person who is ill have the best possible experience. Additionally, there are pragmatic tools, especially related to communication, that can benefit everyone when dealing with doctors.

The "Manic" Culture of Medicine

I noticed high energy and lack of emotion when I first started working in hospitals and outpatient clinics. Not only was it shocking that everyone around me literally moved so much faster than I did, but it was equally unsettling that when talking with a physician, I found that I had about twenty seconds to say what was on my mind before being interrupted! Indeed, some research has found that patients have an average of eighteen seconds to speak before a physician interrupts with a yes or no question.[1] Though patience and emotional connection seem to be in short supply in encounters with physicians, there is an abundance of irritability. Most doctors approach conversations by wanting people to get to the point, and fast. In some ways, an emphasis on speed and conciseness makes sense; in many medical situations urgency can mean the difference between life and death. However, this is rarely the case in primary care or other outpatient medical offices, and it is not clear why people need to be moving quite so quickly. Nevertheless, increased physical and mental activity, a tendency to downplay emotional concerns, and irritability all contribute to what I loosely refer to as the "manic" culture of medicine.

As a consequence of the fast-moving nature of medicine, there is little room for the emotional reactions of patients. A study in Canada found that doctors failed an empathy test in 90 percent of cases.[2] Though this is only one study and many physicians are indeed empathic, the author of the study points out that many physicians have difficulty acknowledging emotions expressed by patients. Many people I know would agree with this assessment. Patients have reported to me over the years that once they became tearful, their physician changed the subject or ended the meeting abruptly! Though I recognize how incredibly painful it is for someone to let their guard down with a physician, only to be cut off, I think it is important to remember that modern medical clinicians are largely disconnected from their own emotions while at work. This may not be a bad thing. Though it is reasonable to wish that the people we entrust to take care of our bodies should also take care of our minds, this may not be possible and should not be taken personally. In fact, some have made the case that doctors' or surgeons' detachment from emotions allows them to continue to do their work every day. The authors of a British publication, *Clinical Counselling in Medical Settings*, argue that the kind of compartmentalization that occurs in medicine can be adaptive; doctors can be detached, and those of us trained in psychology can deal with emotional needs.[3]

Doctor detachment has some advantages. When doctors are somewhat removed, they can evaluate patients objectively, and certainly it is easier to provide intrusive and often painful medical procedures. Consider if your surgeon were overly concerned about cutting you! They might not be able to focus on getting the procedure right if they are consumed with worry. Additionally, a lot of traumatic experiences occur in medical practice: young people hit with random illness, car accidents, victims of violent crime, and so on. These traumas, which are witnessed every day by (initially) often young physicians or physicians in training, can drain and frighten even the most hearty young doctor. At some point, becoming relatively disengaged serves as a valuable survival instinct in the face of dealing with constant traumatic events.

Maybe it is just too much to ask that doctors do everything. After all, in our personal lives, we don't expect any one person to have it all. We have neighbors who are walking partners, colleagues in our book group, associates from religious activities, and friends whom we can talk with about emotional aspects of our lives. In other words, rarely do we find one person who can meet all of our needs. It may not be realistic to think we can find a physician who can do it all.

Talking with Physicians

If I could name the most common complaint I hear from all of the people I see who encounter medical professionals, it is that doctors don't listen. My response to this complaint, after acknowledging how frustrating it can be to talk with physicians, is to say, "Doctors do listen; it's just that they listen in a particular way, and since these conversations don't seem normal, it's hard for us to adjust." I don't say this to defend physicians or to downplay realistic concerns. It's just that most of the physicians I know do care deeply about their patients and want to help. However, the normal rules of social conversation don't exist in the world of medicine. Doctors think fast and move fast, so they want us to reach our conversational conclusions rapidly as well. Therefore, discussions with doctors need to be handled thoughtfully. Many people imagine that physicians are curious and eager to listen to us. Though this is an understandable wish, it is often not true. Doctors do tend to be curious people, but they are also busy and focused on results. It is reasonable that we want to tell our story, but most physicians are dealing with a number of pressing concerns. If we are okay or are doing what we need to do, then there is an assumption that we don't need extended conversations.

For example, I was recently talking with my own doctor regarding very good lab results. I was so pleased that I wanted to tell my doctor about all of the changes I had made regarding diet and exercise and how I might have influenced the results of my tests. My eagerness was met with a polite but fairly dismissive response. My doctor did not want to hear about the nuances of what I had figured out, in terms of diet, to lower my cholesterol. I can appreciate where she is coming from. I am one of hundreds of patients; my doctor just wants to know if I am fine, not what unique dietary trick worked for me. She does not have time for that. Since I did not take our interaction personally, I was not offended. In fact, I was amused at my desire to both please and explain myself to her! However, a number of patients I have seen throughout the years have been insulted during interactions with physicians in which they felt they were not given the time and attention they thought they deserved. Such an attitude can cause problems for both patients and family members.

Don't get me wrong; there is nothing unusual in wishing that a physician be a good listener as well as a good diagnostician. It is just that such a wish, in the current climate of health care, is largely unrealistic. Those who are trained in medicine are taught to ask certain questions and to listen for specific information. The next time your doctor cuts you off, consider that he or she needs to direct the conversation differently in order to get the information they need to help you.

The New Rules of Modern Medicine

Overall, medicine has changed. Both patients and physicians are largely dissatisfied with medical care.[4] Despite ideas that many of us have grown up with, it is rough to be a doctor these days. Physicians often feel overworked and underpaid. Especially in primary care, doctors are paid less than specialist physicians. Additionally, although some older generations still respect physician authority, a newer generation of savvy Internet users has changed the dynamic in patient-physician relationships. Some patients feel that they can diagnose their ailments online and show up at their doctor's office "knowing" what is wrong with them and expecting a specific prescription. In this way, physician authority is questioned in a way that is novel.

In addition, managed care is also a frequent contributor in how medicine has changed and has impacted physician authority. For example, procedures that are deemed necessary by physicians often need prior authorization from an insurance company, who may argue that the procedure or test is not necessary.

However, the story of what has happened to physicians and the culture of medicine is a lot more complicated than changes in health care finances. One hundred years ago, medical clinicians had little to offer patients in the way of actual cures. Instead, they relied on what they had at their disposal and old-fashioned bedside manner. In other words, they simply talked to patients. This worked to some extent. We know now that trust in physicians and their abilities can be very healing. For example, patients who trust physicians and feel that their doctors know them well are more compliant with medical advice.[5] However, changes throughout the last several decades have altered the way that physicians and patients interact. Modern medicine now offers drugs, blood analysis, surgeries, and diagnostic procedures. These advances have put technology at the forefront of medical encounters. Think your general practitioner knows it all? Let's wait and see what your blood tests say. Think your cardiologist might have some ideas about whether or not you have heart disease? Wait until he or she completes a cardiac catheterization, just to be sure. Technology has stepped up as the new expert. While there is still a great art in the practice of medicine, with the knowledge of physicians being the most important aspect of all, practitioners of medicine today are relegated to routine exams, often followed by lab work and advanced medical procedures. This scenario helps patients because everyone benefits from technological advances. But when technology erodes the impact of the patient-physician relationship, everybody suffers.

Technology has changed the entire landscape of medicine and life in general. Whereas once our life expectancy was around fifty-four years of age, we now face a life span of much more than that, with recent statistics suggesting that many of us could become centenarians. Simply put, our longer lives and sheer numbers are overwhelming the health care system. As much as this frustrates us, imagine how hard it is for physicians. Doctors may have gone into the field to prolong life, but now life is longer than any of us ever imagined. They have more elderly patients, more sick patients, and more patients in general to take care of. That is just the beginning of how things have changed.

Algorithms and actuarial data now replace the personal attention that people used to get: mammograms at age forty, colonoscopies at fifty, make sure the box is checked. This is the reality of primary care medicine today. For those of us who are healthy, we simply need to go to the doctor and make sure all of the boxes are checked.

But what if someone has a serious medical problem? How do you make sure neither you nor your loved one falls into the abyss of primary care algorithms? This is a culture in which we need to do more work as patients or patient advocates to make sure we are getting the attention we need.

It is more important than ever to be aware of the rules of medicine. We can have good relationships with doctors, but in order to get the most from them, we have to abide by their often unspoken cultural demands. This is not unlike visiting another country and respecting the importance of trying to speak the language and act like the locals. Consider the following rules as your guide when you visit the foreign and strange world of medicine:

The Rules of Modern Medicine

1. Time is in short supply
2. Discussions should be concise
3. Emotions are generally discouraged
4. Patients are supposed to be compliant
5. Questions are tolerated but not overtly encouraged
6. Though some physicians try to incorporate a collaborative model, most still expect to be the authority
7. Responsibility for health lies within the patient
8. Aggression tends to be expressed more directly
9. Uncertainty is generally not tolerated

As these rules suggest, it is easier to acculturate to medicine when we keep our emotions in check. There is one caveat, however. Though vulnerable emotions are not encouraged when interacting with medical clinicians, there is a surprising tolerance for assertiveness. In fact, some research has suggested that being assertive is crucial to getting needs met from a doctor. A study of patients interacting with physicians found that patients who were assertive received more supportive and informative communication from doctors.[6] In fact, a lot of research has shown that patients who feel entitled to express frustration and articulate preferences have a positive impact in medical encounters. This may seem counterintuitive, but it makes sense given the culture of medicine. Doctors tend to take over when patients are passive; they simply provide directions and move on to the next patient. The lesson in this is that a healthy sense of entitlement is key. Ask for what you need, and it is okay to feel confident that you can have questions answered or even complain a little when needs are not being met.

The Medical Consultation

The best way to approach an appointment with a physician is to treat it like a business meeting. Have an idea of what you want to achieve during the appointment. This cannot be overstated. Structure is incredibly important in medical training. Doctors have a list of things they need to take care of in any medical visit, often before they even walk in the door. You should have your own list to be sure that your needs are met as well. Understandably, when talking with a doctor about a scary diagnosis, it is difficult to stay focused. This is why it is good to write down your questions or new symptoms before the appointment. If possible, email or fax the list to your doctor ahead of time. Have a hard copy with you at the appointment and give it to your doctor when she or he walks in the door. These pragmatic strategies are important because they match well with how physicians are trained; you are presenting your goals and objectives for the meeting.

You may not have that much time in your actual appointment. This is where being concise is most helpful. Keep questions and thoughts brief, and focus on what is most important. Your list should be short. Sometimes people have long lists and a lot of questions. This is okay, but you may need to schedule another appointment in order to get through everything. If your problems are complex or you have a lot you want to go over, ask that your next appointment be longer. Most people don't know that they can ask for a thirty-minute appointment instead of a fifteen-minute one.

Many patients and family members have questions that come up between appointments. As you likely already know, it can be hard to get in touch with a doctor, and waiting for a call back can feel like an eternity. The number one thing I tell people dealing with this dilemma is to call your doctor (email if you can), communicate your question, and if you don't hear back within a day or two, call again. I have rarely heard a physician complain about a couple of phone or email messages. In fact, if they have forgotten about a call or message, they usually appreciate the reminder to call back. Complaints arise, however, when patients call or email multiple times a day, because doctors often schedule their callbacks during certain times. Multiple attempts at contact can irritate your physician, and irritated physicians are less likely to return phone calls or emails. A power struggle can ensue in which a physician feels pressured, which may trigger further procrastination on his or her part. Moderation is key when trying to get in touch with doctors; too little risks falling under the radar screen and too much risks alienation.

Often the key to getting in touch with a physician is contact with the unsung heroes in medical offices: the staff. Medical personnel are key players in the world of doctors and good relationships with them are crucial. It is important to remember that these people also often feel underpaid and overworked, and we need to express patience and understanding with them as well. Receptionists, medical assistants, and nurses do not have the ultimate authority in medicine. Yet they do provide a direct pipeline and have the ear of the physicians we are trying to reach. Therefore, you can apply some of the same rules in dealing with them that you apply with doctors. If you call a receptionist and yell or act rudely, don't think that the doctor won't hear about it. Not only that, but patients who mistreat medical staff can quickly gain a reputation of being "difficult." Such a label is a bad situation in medicine; patients who are labeled this way do not receive the level of care that they need and deserve. Think of it this way: anything you may say to a medical staff person is like talking with your doctor. You don't want to alienate the people from whom you need help. This includes everyone from the receptionist to the medical assistant, the nurse, and your physician.

Keep in mind that in this day and age of large medical offices, the main phone number that you call to make an appointment may not be located on the same site (or even the same state!) as your medical office. Some medical offices centralize or outsource to other areas to save costs. So while you may think that you are communicating with someone who will actually see your doctor that day, you may not be, and this is a bit more like calling an answering service. If you are having trouble getting in contact with your doctor, find out where you are calling. If you discover that your doctor in California has calls directed to a service in Texas, ask for a direct number to her or his medical assistant or nurse. Most physicians don't mind these requests. Remember that your physician may not always be getting your messages or know how important your call is. Ask your doctor face to face what the best way is to get in touch if something important arises.

Managing Emotions in the Doctor's Office

Doctors do not generally embrace ambiguity and uncertainty in their behavior or the behavior of others. Therefore, be clear about your questions. This does not mean that you cannot have uncertain or conflicted feelings. However, while you may have all kinds of complicated feelings, addressing them in a doctor's office is usually not going to satisfy you. Patients frequently report to me that they tried to talk with their doctor about emotional issues and these conversations were disappointing. Though doctors often do listen, emotional discussions simply require more time, which is rarely available. One way some physicians handle emotional issues is to direct a patient's emotional concerns to a therapist. This can be extremely frustrating to patients who do not feel they need therapy. Yet, such referrals are often not inappropriate; most sensitive physicians recognize the limitations of their time and abilities. If you consider a medical consultation as a business meeting, then it makes all the more sense to compartmentalize complex emotions until you are with someone who is more available to hear them.

That being said, when it comes to issues of diagnostic uncertainty, it is important to be clear if you are worried about something. As author Jerome Groopman describes in his bestselling book *How Doctors Think*, if you are worried that you are being misdiagnosed, say something.[7] Groopman describes a patient saying something like, "I am most worried that what seemed like acid reflux could be the first sign of cancer." Such statements may make you feel vulnerable but can help let your physician know that you want to make sure all possibilities are being considered in his or her understanding of what is wrong with you. In other words, it is more than okay to let your doctor know that you are worried that something is being missed. Doctors get it right most of the time, but sometimes they make mistakes, so feel free to speak up if you think they are getting something wrong.

On a related note, you should also get a second opinion if you have questions and possibly even if you do not. We can feel intimidated in seeking out another opinion, but it is crucial that medical patients or advocates feel entitled to confirm or question a diagnosis. As Groopman describes, doctors get it right 80 percent of the time. This is good news for most of us, yet no one wants to be in the 20 percent of people who are misdiagnosed. I always tell people that if symptoms are not responding to treatment, or even if they are but a medical condition is complex or rare, it is worth seeing another specialist. Doctors do not typically take second opinions personally or, if they do, they are professional enough to manage their emotions about this. If a doctor has a problem with your seeking a second opinion, you should question whether or not you want this person to provide your care. An overly sensitive physician may be difficult to work with in the long run and may be resistant to questions or concerns as medical issues progress. Everyone needs a doctor who can handle questions and concerns.

I realize that some of my recommendations run the risk of placing patients in subordinate status. It may sound as if I am saying that we should simply accept our status as devalued consumers who need doctors more than they need us. Though I certainly don't believe that we should allow ourselves to be mistreated, years of talking with patients and physicians have taught me that there is a game to be played when dealing with doctors. Most physicians mean well but are overworked. Some are even frustrated that their chosen career is not more satisfying. But even more relevant is that in reality, each of us is one of many. Doctors have a lot of patients. While we might wish we were more important than other patients, we usually are not. Though physicians have a lot of difficulties in terms of how they communicate, one issue that patients often bring to the medical encounter is that they want to be treated as if they are someone special. The sad reality is that no matter what we or loved ones may be going through, our situations are not special in the world of medicine. The problems we have are unique and special to us, but when doctors have hundreds of patients, our problems are not unique to them. We all need to deal with this reality. This is where seeking the help of psychotherapy can be useful.

CHAPTER 3
COPING CHECKLIST

- Treat appointments with doctors like a business meeting. Have an agenda. Plan what you are going to say to the doctor ahead of time.
- Since you may be interrupted, mention the most serious issues first. If there are multiple issues, say, "We have three things we need you to know."
- If you have questions, write them down. Ask if you can fax or email questions to your doctor ahead of time.
- If you can't get your questions to a doctor ahead of time, put questions on paper. Hand it to your doctor when he or she first walks in and say, "Here is what we need answered before we leave."
- If your appointments feel too short, ask for a longer appointment next time. Many people don't know that they can ask for a thirty-minute follow-up as opposed to a standard fifteen-minute visit.
- Feel entitled to express your needs. Be assertive if you need to.
- If you need to be in touch with your doctor between appointments and have not received a call back, keep calling; doctors are often not offended by multiple calls.
- If you have not heard back from your doctor in a day or two, ask the office staff if you can fax or email a note to the doctor.
- Use your face-to-face contact with your doctor to find out what the best way is to get in touch if something important arises.
- Be sure to tell the office staff how much you

appreciate their time and energy. If you have the financial resources, bring them a gift like a fruit basket or a pound of candy during your next visit, so they remember you.

- Don't be afraid to get a second opinion. If your doctor has a problem with this, consider getting a new doctor.

Notes

1. T. Realini, A. Kalert, and J. Sparling, "Interruption in the Medical Interaction," *Archives of Internal Medicine* 4 (1995): 1028–33.
2. "Doctors fail empathy test in 90% of cases: Chaplains can help," *Healthcare Chaplaincy Today.* Accessed May 28, 2011, http://www.healthcarechaplaincy.org/about-us/enewsletter/issue-26-february-2011.html#1.
3. P. Thomas, S. Davison, and C. Rance, eds. *Clinical Counselling in Medical Settings* (New York: Taylor and Francis, 2001).
4. A. Zuger, "Dissatisfaction with medical practice," *New England Journal of Medicine* 350 (2004): 69–75.
5. G. Cousin, and M.S. Mast, "Agreeable patient meets affiliative physician: How physician behavior affects patient outcomes depends on patient personality," *Patient Education and Counseling* (in press), doi:10.1016/j.pec.2011.02.010.
6. R.L. Street, H.S. Gordon, M.M. Ward, E. Krupat, and R.L. Kravitz, "Patient participation in medical consultations: Why some patients are more involved than others," *Medical Care* 43 (2005): 960–69.
7. J. Groopman, *How Doctors Think* (New York: Houghton Mifflin, 2007).

chapter four

MANAGING DENIAL

When someone we care about gets hit with a serious illness, it can be hard to take in. Loved ones often initially experience shock and disbelief. Illness, even when it occurs in someone else's body, stirs up a great deal of anxiety and helplessness in all of us. When these feelings are too much to bear, disbelief can take over. Denial can wreak havoc not just on the person who is sick but on the lives of their loved ones as well. This is to be expected. But if you remain in a state of disbelief, you will be unable to support your loved one. And when patients are in denial about illness, the consequences can be even more devastating. Though short-term denial can be beneficial, long-term denial can lead to neglect of one's body. Not following medical advice is risky. Noncompliance can exacerbate illness and increase chances of death, which affects not just the patient but also everyone who wants to see the patient live as long and as well as possible.

This chapter will discuss how anxiety and helplessness

can result in denial when they are not properly addressed. Excessive denial can create a system in which patients engage in increasingly self-destructive behaviors, while loved ones either stand by helplessly or ignore what is happening. Although spouses, friends, and family often feel powerless, they have more influence than they know. In fact, the quality of close relationships has a powerful impact on health. Supportive relationships protect against the development of illness, and relationships that are antagonistic can put people at risk for disease. The key for us as loved ones is to find a balance between engaging in behaviors that may have a positive influence and knowing that there are limits to how much we can control.

The Anxious Terrain of Illness:
When the Patient Is in Denial

When illness strikes, we often feel disoriented. We all are accustomed to the lives we have with those we love: our mothers might call us on Fridays with updates, we have familiar routines with our spouses, we get together with certain friends around the same time each month. When illness affects someone we care about, not only do these routines change, but life for everyone changes as well.

The fact of illness, that our bodies and minds can fail us, makes us all incredibly anxious. Most of us would prefer not to think about such things at all. So, despite what can be obvious changes when someone gets sick, it is tempting to ignore reality. This temptation is often stronger when the patient seems to be dismissing symptoms. When a close friend of mine was diagnosed with a rare autoimmune disorder, she dismissed her symptoms, which were quite physically apparent. I felt scared about what was happening to her and awkward in terms of how to talk about it. I found myself unsure if I should ask about her obvious physical changes. It seemed that since she was ignoring her symptoms, then I should too. In this way, denial can be contagious. However, not asking also felt false to me, and then I worried that I was not being attentive as a friend.

When people are in denial, we, as friends or family, are in a terrible bind: wanting to help but not wanting to intrude. Indeed, patients sometimes complain about being asked about their illness. Not asking, however, risks sending the message that we do not want to hear about what is happening. Such binds are common and often reflect the true anxiety and ambivalence patients themselves feel about discussing their illness. Consider the Showtime series *The Big C*, in which the main character, Cathy, has been diagnosed with Stage IV melanoma. In the first season, she seems to want to tell those around her, including her husband, Paul, but then finds that Paul and other family members are so limited that she can't quite make herself vulnerable enough to share her terrible news. Cathy's lack of disclosure is couched in her disappointment with her loved ones; her husband is insensitive, her brother's life is a mess, and her son is a teenager with other concerns. This is not an inaccurate portrayal of how some people with illness express a form of denial. Patients sometimes focus on character flaws in others and assume they won't be able to handle hearing about illness. However, such beliefs about the limitations of others are often a protective mechanism and have more to do with the psychology of the patient than the limitations of loved ones. When patients don't tell others about their illness, it is often a way they try to manage their own

overwhelming feelings. Not telling others reflects a wish
to ignore the truth: if others don't know, then this can't be
happening. As with many things in life that are difficult
to bear emotionally, problems seem much more real when
we say them out loud.

I once saw a patient, whom I will call Beth, who had
a severe form of cancer. She told literally no one, not even
her husband or her children. When I asked what she did
when she went through chemotherapy and lost her hair,
she said, "I just wore wigs." To her credit, at least this
woman was not so much in denial that she avoided her
medical treatment. However, though she went through
the motions of chemotherapy, on some level she needed
to pretend to herself and others that this was not happening. It may seem hard to believe, but based on how the
human psyche works, we can all have two separate states
of mind that hold opposite beliefs or realities. Consider
this from another angle: Millions of people smoke cigarettes even though they are aware of the dangers. On one
level, they know they are engaging in a dangerous behavior. However, most smokers maintain a sense of denial:
the negative consequences of smoking won't happen to
them. This is also true when people are ill. Denial can
exist in a separate part of the mind as well. The purpose
of denial is to keep people from being overwhelmed by
feelings. This can have some benefit early in illness, as
being overwhelmed can interfere with the need to mobilize coping resources. In the long run, though, denial
does not work. Smokers experience negative health consequences, whether they believe it or not. In Beth's case,
she paid a high psychological price for her denial. Her
family knew something was wrong. They just didn't feel
like they could talk about it. This took a tremendous toll

on the family. Her children started acting out, her husband became distant, and she felt isolated from all of her friends, which was why she sought therapy. Denial starts out as a form of protection but can become destructive.

Anxiety and Helplessness: When the Person in Denial Is You

Patients who are in denial about illness unintentionally place an enormous burden on loved ones. But loved ones can experience their own denial. Once we find out that someone close to us is ill, we need to manage our own emotions in order to be as supportive as possible.

When someone we care about is sick, we often feel helpless. This is a normal response and one I would encourage you to acknowledge rather than try to get away from. Many people tell me that helplessness is the most horrid of emotions because they feel they can do nothing with it. Of course this is true; helplessness means just that. Helplessness is feeling out of control, with a tremendous desire to take an active stance.

The desire to do something can be channeled productively. We can call sick friends more often, we can remind spouses to take medications; we can help our parents with finances. When we learn to tolerate feelings of helplessness, it allows us to think more clearly about what we can do to be supportive. However, some people are so destabilized by feelings of helplessness they decide to act in ways that are not helpful to themselves or patients. They may get angry and demand action from doctors or medical clinicians. When loved ones argue with people providing care, it is often related to an inability to manage overwhelming feelings.

Alison had recently moved her mother into a well-reputed assisted living facility after she had been diagnosed with dementia. Alison was heartbroken to see her mother decline physically and psychologically. When Alison's mother had lived at home, she used to call Alison several times a day in a confused state, asking questions that Alison had answered in previous phone calls. Although on some level Alison was relieved that her mother had more help and would not be alone, she felt completely unprepared for the eventuality of her mother's death.

Additionally, Alison worried a great deal about her own health. Her mother's dementia signaled to her that she, too, would have to bear the burden of this horrible illness. But instead of being able to manage these worries and feelings, Alison became overly focused on what she assumed to be poor care that her mother was receiving. She visited her mother every day at the facility and complained about nearly every aspect of her mother's care. Though all relatives want to ensure good care for family members, Alison's complaints were excessive. For example, she complained that food in the facility was not good enough, even though her mother indicated that she liked the food and ate whatever was served to her. She thought the staff was not attentive enough, though they checked in on her mother frequently. Alison resorted to calling or seeing the director of the facility several times a week to complain. The director assured her that her mother was adjusting well, but he eventually became exasperated with Alison's complaints.

Alison's situation is a good example of how people try to distract themselves from overwhelming feelings. Although most children worry about the care parents are receiving in any facility, Alison was trying to manage her helplessness and anxiety by focusing on the shortcomings of the staff. Such distractions usually do not work. When she finally realized that her mother was fine and, in fact, thriving in her new home, Alison had to question her intensity toward the staff. She came to understand that she was trying to manage her feelings of helplessness by trying to take control of her mother's care. Ironically, Alison had already done such a good job of helping her mother out that her mother was just fine. It was much harder for Alison to deal with her feelings about losing the mother she had known all of her life and to start thinking about her mother's eventual death.

Coping with loss involves coming to terms with being helpless. Sometimes, in the face of their own feelings of helplessness, people even get mad at the person who is ill, and they end up making unreasonable demands given the patient's true physical limitations. For example, many children of people with dementia describe feeling angry that their parents appear weak or vulnerable. Such expressions are not uncommon. When we feel helpless, we often look to others to make things better, just like we did when we were children and turned to our parents. When we look for a solution from the person who has a physical illness, however, that person can often do little to help us. We are left to our own devices. Feeling alone in this way is hard for loved ones to bear. Consider the case of Mark:

Mark was twenty-six years old when he sought therapy after his mother had been diagnosed with leukemia. He acknowledged how hard it had been to see her go through a bone marrow transplant and was relieved to talk with someone about his experience. His mother's prognosis remained uncertain, although her health had been stable in recent months. He found himself irritable at work and unable to connect with his girlfriend. He felt angry and distant with her and often wished he was somewhere else when they were together. In regard to his mother, he noted that although he spent a great deal of time with her while she was in the hospital, now that she was home, he found excuses to avoid visiting her. When he did see her, he was troubled by how annoyed he felt at her need for help.

Mark's situation illustrates the ways that feelings of irritability and anger can hide feelings of helplessness. As I got to know Mark, it was clear he was terrified of his mother's potential health decline, but this feeling was masked by crankiness toward the two most important women in his life. Often, anger and irritability are easier to express than fear, sadness, grief, and helplessness. This is why so many people experience anger in the face of illness. Anger is organizing. When we are angry, we can identify a "bad guy." In Mark's case, the bad guys were his girlfriend and his mother's expression of her vulnerability. In illness, the real bad guy is the disease that is ravaging the patient's body. As an outsider, there is no way to fight it. So helplessness ensues and angry feelings are mobilized. However, anger is usually a futile weapon in the face of illness; it does little to protect the ones we love. Additionally, though anger may seem to be an antidote to helplessness, anger does not take this feeling away. In fact, it can make it worse. When we act angry, we may engage in behaviors that hurt others. When we don't maintain good control of how we act, or engage in ways that we later regret, we end up feeling more helpless!

Coming to terms with how scared we are can go a long way in helping to deal with feelings of anger and irritability. For Mark, he needed to realize that he felt powerless to help his mother, who had raised him as a single parent and who had been so strong in his eyes throughout his childhood. Realizing that he was terrified about his mother's illness and her not recovering helped him to be less touchy with his girlfriend, and he was eventually able to confide in her about his fears, which made them both feel closer to one another. He also found it easier to be with his mother and to offer her practical help and emotional support when she needed it.

When Denial Leads to Noncompliance

While research suggests that denial early in illness can help prevent patients from being overwhelmed with feelings,[1] extended denial can be harmful to both physical and psychological health. The most problematic outcome of denial is that it can lead to disregarding medical advice. Noncompliance, sometimes referred to as nonadherence, is when patients either do not do what a doctor has prescribed or continue to engage in behaviors that can cause or exacerbate illness.

Noncompliance is extremely common. Estimates vary depending on the study but range from 25 to 50 percent of patients.[2] If your loved one is not taking medications as prescribed, continues to smoke, or drinks too much, they are not alone. Although people's treatment of their bodies is highly personal, when loved ones are invested in helping someone get better or manage illness, self-care impacts everyone. When patients do not take care of themselves, it places a large burden on those around them, who may feel that they have no choice but to helplessly witness self-destruction.

Self-care is hard, and the guidelines for what all of

us are supposed to do to take care of ourselves can feel overwhelming. For example, current recommendations on optimal self-care include eating large amounts of fruits and vegetables, managing weight, minimizing sugar, consuming less red meat, getting frequent exercise, seeing a dentist every six months, limiting alcohol, and getting good, quality sleep for 7–9 hours a night. Medications need to be taken regularly. Even having a pet has been found to improve health! For most people, these ideal guidelines require energy and resources that are unavailable or hard to find. For example, when I talk with college students who have to work as well as study, suggesting they find time to exercise is often met with a polite but dismissive laugh. Additionally, self-care can be expensive. Nutritious foods are often more expensive than unhealthy foods. Pets, while enjoyable, require a fair amount of money. Imagine telling someone who can barely feed her children to buy a dog! Yet there are people who have time and financial resources to follow medical advice, and they do not. A related consequence of our tendency to deny death is to ignore the risks of certain behaviors.

That said, there is a difference between taking health risks when one is well versus when one is facing a medical crisis. There is an expectation that when someone becomes ill they will stop doing things that are harmful and follow all medical advice about taking medications, attending appointments, completing diagnostic tests, and so on. In ideal situations, illness can be a wake-up call to attend to one's body. For some, illness does not provide such motivation. Sometimes people even engage in more self-destructive behaviors. Consider the situation of Josephine and her husband of thirty years, Bill:

Josephine sought therapy after her husband, Bill, had a heart attack. She was worried about her husband's refusal to change his lifestyle behaviors. He kept smoking cigarettes, refused to exercise, and did not take his medications as prescribed. Additionally, Josephine's husband began drinking heavily. Although she had tried to talk with him about some of his health behaviors, it always resulted in a fight. Bill accused Josephine of being nagging and controlling, and Josephine worried that her husband might have another heart attack and die. Though she hated Bill's accusations that she was overly attentive to his health behaviors, Josephine acknowledged that every time Bill smoked, she complained. She also noted that her comments to Bill seemed to cause him to smoke more.

There is perhaps no state of helplessness that can match when someone we love does not do what is needed for self-care. On one level, we could say that people's treatment of their bodies is their business. On the other hand, when someone we love is ill, their treatment of their body can feel quite personal to us. As I got to know Josephine, it was clear that she not only genuinely worried about her husband's health but also took Bill's noncompliance personally. She considered it an insult that he did not listen to her, and she thought that if he loved her more, he would take better care of his body so that they could remain together.

Although Josephine's reaction was normal, such a response can cause a great deal of suffering. Ideas about a spouse's noncompliance are usually not accurate. Spouses often worry that a patient's noncompliance reflects their feelings about the relationship. When people do not take care of themselves, it has to do with a number of complicated variables, which usually have to do with only themselves.

For example, people who are depressed are much less likely to take medications as prescribed.[3] In fact, depression is a major factor in why patients do not follow medical advice. Additionally, people who worry about being dependent on others and who are terrified of death tend to fall into the trap of noncompliance. Illness and death are so frightening for some people that they actually engage in self-destructive behaviors as a way of controlling how and when they will die. This may not make intuitive sense, but think about it through the lens of control. For some people, a lack of control is terrifying. This can stem from more than just fears about their present illness; much of it can go all the way back to childhood. One well-known study found that people who had abusive and chaotic childhoods are more likely to abuse alcohol and drugs and engage in risky sexual behavior.[4] Child abuse also makes it difficult for people to regulate and manage emotions. When people abuse alcohol or drugs or use cigarettes, it can sometimes be related to attempts to manage overwhelming feelings. Substances become a way to self-medicate mood. Additionally, not taking care of one's body can paradoxically be a way that people can try to gain control. People who engage in self-destructive behaviors are often aware of what they are doing to themselves physically. But anxiety about illness and death can paradoxically lead to taking control in unhealthy ways. Often an underlying reason for this has to do with a fear of illness or death, such as when a smoker says, "I know I shouldn't smoke, but something's gonna kill me!"

The threat of illness makes some people feel out of control. In my experience, fears of illness are more pronounced in those who have had chaotic, unpredictable, and abusive childhoods. Though it seems logical that someone would want to do everything they can to improve their chance of survival, often people feel so worried about illness and death that they paradoxically engage in behaviors that are likely to cause it.

Illness can be so frightening, some patients may feel a sense of helplessness and hopelessness about taking care of themselves. This feeling is often expressed as, "I am going to die anyway, so why should I do things that will help? It won't change anything." People feel powerless when they are depressed and often lack the energy needed for self-care. This is why treating depression can be an important first step in helping someone who is noncompliant.

The Impact of Relationships on Noncompliant Patients

A young woman recently complained about her boyfriend's use of cocaine and how it might make him vulnerable to illness. She accurately worried about the impact of cocaine on his heart. However, pointing this out seemed to have an opposite effect of what she hoped. Her partner accused her of being uptight, and he used the drug more when she complained about it. Knowing what to do in these situations can be tricky, but managing our own emotions can help us approach those we love with both tact and concern. Perhaps the number one thing we can tell ourselves is that ultimately, we can't control how other people treat their bodies.

Although it is true that we can't make people treat their bodies better, loved ones can have positive or negative influences on compliance. It turns out that stressful and conflict-filled relationships may be bad for health.

An analysis of 122 studies found that when patients feel emotionally supported by spouses and family members, they are more likely to comply with medical advice.[5] Alternatively, conflict reduces the likelihood that patients will take care of themselves.

The quality of relationships affects more than just compliance. The stress of adverse interactions can have negative consequences on health. One study found that people reporting negative aspects of close relationships (such as conflict and arguing) were more likely to develop heart disease.[6] Another study found that distress in spouses predicted the worsening of symptoms in patients with heart failure.[7] In both of these studies, self-care did not explain the results. In other words, though problematic relationships may contribute to noncompliance, there are also likely physiological effects of long-term antagonistic and unsupportive relationships.

Although the implications of this are scary, the findings of these studies make sense. We have known for quite some time that social support can improve health. Additionally, we know that long-term depression, anxiety, and feelings of hostility can have negative health consequences. It seems intuitive that when our relationships are stressful, it could exacerbate depression and anxiety. Further, relationships that are high in conflict can leave us carrying around angry and hostile feelings. Put quite simply, negative feelings, when they persist, are not good for our minds or our bodies.

What we can do is manage our own negative feelings in relationships, take control where we can, and try not to escalate the situation into something that becomes highly conflicted. The way to do this is to not take noncompliance personally. When we take things personally, we tend to overreact and try to get control in ways that are counterproductive.

When Denial Works as a System

Particularly in families, denial can be a team effort. There are times when loved ones simply give up on trying to change a patient and go along with however a patient wants to act. Most of you are no doubt familiar with the terms "codependence" and "enabling." This is what I am referring to. For example, a man I will call John had diabetes and continued to eat large quantities of sugar. His wife, Janice, who was also not in great health, used to make him desserts that he could enjoy. In this case, simply talking with John about his eating habits was not enough to help him. I had the chance to see both John and his wife to talk about how she might have an impact on John's eating habits. It was clear when I talked with the couple that they both were in denial about the seriousness of John's condition. Though they both stated that they intellectually understood the risks of John not managing his blood sugar, emotionally, they were unprepared to change anything. John's wife was an excellent cook, and she enjoyed being in what she viewed as a caretaking role. It took several meetings to convince them that Janice could continue to take care of her husband in a more positive way. Since Janice loved to cook and John loved to eat, we discussed several ways Janice could cook and bake lower carbohydrate foods for John. Interestingly, once Janice signed on to a plan of helping him, John began to take more charge of his diet and was more attentive to what he ate, as well as to monitoring his blood sugar levels.

When denial works as a system, all parties involved

are buying the same message: the patient's body is working fine and we do not have to do anything differently.
Chances are if you are reading this book, you are likely
not in denial. However, we all have ways that we can
become part of a system of denial without realizing it.
Spouses ignore behaviors that make them anxious, and
we can all make excuses for why people don't take care
of themselves. For example, a woman might say of her
husband who has not been to the doctor in ten years, "He
is just too busy to go to the doctor. He is still relatively
young and healthy. He will go when he needs to." Such
justifications have some utility. They keep us from feeling
helpless. Knowing how and when to confront noncompliance and lack of self-care is as awkward as it is complicated. The reality is there may not be anything you can
do to change how someone you love treats his or her body.
But you can try to discuss your thoughts and feelings. By
doing so, you will have a greater idea of your actual (and
not imagined) influence.

Confronting Denial and Noncompliance

Denial in patients can be very taxing to family
members or friends who often carry the true burden of
a patient's denial; they are aware of what is happening
to the patient but feel helpless to do anything about it.
However, when patients are in denial, family members
or friends may simply go along with the story a patient
is trying to create. Confronting a patient's denial is scary
and can lead to conflict.

Denial is often a reaction to fear and reflects the terror
not only of death but also of being limited and having
to depend on others. As witnesses to denial, loved ones
can feel helpless, but there are ways to cautiously confront

denial. First, the patient who is in denial often wishes, even if in secret, that others know about their illness or confront their denial. After all, denying illness and attempting to ignore the impact of noncompliance takes a large amount of emotional energy. That being said, subtlety goes a long way when trying to talk with someone in denial; for example, you could say to a friend who may have been avoiding you because of illness, "You have been on my mind. Is everything okay?"

But people with illness don't necessarily avoid friends. They have symptoms, which might be noticeable, yet they continue to interact with others as if nothing is wrong. In such situations, it is worth saying something like, "I know this might be uncomfortable to bring up, but I have noticed that you might not be feeling as well as you often do." While it might seem that being so subtle risks coming off as patronizing, remember that people who are not discussing illness or who are in denial are conflicted about whether or not they want to talk about it. The idea in these situations is to open the door a bit and let your friends know that you are mindful of them and their health.

With closer relationships, such as a spouse or parent, this can be even more complicated. When spouses, family, or close personal friends are not taking care of their bodies, it is important to say something. Not speaking up sends the message that you are okay with how they are behaving. People who are noncompliant often wish that a loved one would notice. Sometimes this can be a setup for a fight. For example, I got the sense that Bill secretly did not mind Josephine's complaints because then he had an excuse to be angry at her instead of feeling helpless and sad about his situation. Sometimes all we can do in such situations is express our love and concern. For example, I coached Josephine to tell her husband, "I love you and I am worried about your body. If you need to smoke and not exercise, that is your choice, but I am terrified of you dying because of these behaviors. I don't want to control you but can't imagine how hard life would be without you." Such comments eventually helped Bill get a better handle on his actions and allowed him to consider therapy to help him deal with his feelings about having had a heart attack. This freed up Josephine to recognize that Bill alone was responsible for his body.

We can all feel like children in our marriages sometimes, and we want and need to feel that our spouse cares for us in the way that our parents did (or should have). In that light, it is perfectly understandable that sometimes loved ones need to remind spouses how much they care. All of us need to be reminded how important we are to those we are close to. This is particularly important in long-term relationships. When we are with spouses for years or decades, it may be easy to fall into the routine of assuming that our partners know how we feel. Remember that people who are noncompliant can believe that they do not matter. Sometimes simply acknowledging that you are aware that the person you care about is not paying attention to his or her body can be enough to serve as a wake up call.

You can also try asking questions about health behaviors, such as, "Do you think that if you stopped smoking it might make your symptoms better?" Or, "If you took your medications, would that help you feel better?" However, there can be a fine line between a question asked in a patronizing or antagonistic manner and one that communicates genuine curiosity and interest. Therefore, if you are going to try to ask such a question, consider doing it when a patient is complaining about symptoms and when you are not feeling angry.

Perhaps the most important thing to do when someone you love is ill and not taking care of his or her body is to work together to make positive health changes. This is especially important for spouses, who live together and can heavily influence diet, exercise, and medication compliance. Spouses can engage patients in self-care by suggesting that they exercise together or try new dietary options. For example, if your spouse has heart disease, you could suggest taking a walk together after dinner. If your spouse is diabetic and loves pasta, you could suggest cooking lower carbohydrate pasta, such as whole wheat pasta or soba noodles. Your partner may be unwilling, but encouraging healthy changes will help you feel that you have at least tried to exert control in a positive way.

In terms of actual conversations, the most important thing to remember is not to engage in a fight if you can help it. Remember, anxiety, anger, and depression can be toxic to our own bodies as well as to those we want to support, so discussions should reflect caring and consideration. If you don't take noncompliance and denial personally, this will be much easier. The main tenet of such conversations should be to communicate concern but realize the limits of your control. After all, people have the right to treat their bodies however they choose. As loved ones, we are witnesses and bystanders. Let the person know that you care, are concerned, and want to help.

This strategy can be quite successful. For example, I once knew a couple in which the husband did not take his medications regularly. His wife was concerned about this and gently asked if her husband would be opposed to her reminding him. He was quite open to this. She agreed to remind him to take his medication before they went to bed. Not only did this help him take his medications more regularly, it also helped his wife feel as though she could contribute positively to his overall health and well-being.

Despite our best attempts, however, sometimes the people we care about are not willing to make changes. We all need to figure out how to live with this. The friend I mentioned earlier in the chapter did not take care of her body, continued to ignore her symptoms, and actually avoided our close group of friends. We all called and emailed her multiple times, and she simply avoided us. Though it would be tempting to take this personally, I (as well as my other friends) did not. We understood her need to distance herself from us as a symptom of her denial and her need to avoid those of us who knew about her illness. She needed to pretend that her illness was not real, and that meant cutting out those of us who symbolized the part of herself that knew she was ill. In this situation, all we can do is wait until her denial stops working, and at that point, she will need her friends again. Sometimes waiting is all you can do.

Chapter 4
Coping Checklist

- Acknowledge that illness makes most of us feel helpless. Focus on the ways you have control.
- Communicate concern but realize the limits of your control.
- Don't take noncompliance personally. If the person you care about does not follow medical advice, remember that you are not to blame.
- Conversations should be subtle and not blaming. Say, "I am sorry that this has happened to you and to us. I am scared that you might not beat this illness, but I think if we try together, we can take more control."
- If the person you care about is angry, say, "I totally understand how enraging this is. This illness is not fair, but if you take your medication and do what your doctor says, it might give you more control."
- Remind the patient how much you care. This sounds like a simple idea, but it can be an important reminder of how their illness and the way they treat their bodies affects those they love.
- Depression is a factor in noncompliance. If you think the patient is depressed, urge him or her to seek help.
- When someone you care about does not follow medical advice, try asking questions (when you are not feeling angry or annoyed) about how behaviors may be impacting symptoms. For example, "Do you think that if you stopped smoking it might make your symptoms better?" Or, "If you took your medications, would that help you feel better?"
- Offer to go to doctor appointments with the patient.

- Communicate that no matter what, you plan to be around to help.
- Hang in there. Denial is often (though not always) a temporary state. People need their friends and family when denial subsides.
- If you feel guilty about past relationship issues, remember that the person you care about is likely not thinking about past hurts. What is important is the present.
- Understand that people who are in denial are terrified. They need reassurance, understanding, and love.

Notes

1. D.A. Matt, M.E. Sementilli, T.G. Burish, "Denial as a strategy for coping with cancer," *Journal of Mental Health Counseling* 10, no. 2 (1988): 136–44.
2. M.R. DiMatteo, "Enhancing patient adherence to medical recommendations," *Journal of the American Medical Association* 271 (1994): 79–83; R.B. Haynes, D.L. Sackett, and D.W. Taylor, "Practical management of low compliance with antihypertensive therapy: A guide for the busy practitioner," *Clinical and Investigative Medicine* 1 (1979): 175–80.
3. J.L. Grenard, B.A. Munjas, J.L. Adams, M. Suttorp, M. Maglione, E.A. McGlynn, and W.F. Gellad, "Depression and medication adherence in the treatment of chronic diseases in the United States: A meta-analysis." *Journal of General Internal Medicine*, May 1, 2011, epub ahead of print.
4. V. J. Felitti, R.F. Anda, D. Nordenberg, D.F. Williamson, A.M. Spitz, V. Edwards, et al., "Relationship of childhood abuse and household dysfunction to many leading causes of death in adults," *American Journal of Preventive Medicine* 14, no. 4 (1998): 245–58.
5. M.R. DiMatteo, "Social support and patient adherence to medical treatment: A meta-analysis," *Health Psychology* 23, no. 2 (2004): 207–18.
6. R. De Vogli, T. Chandola, and M.G. Marmot, "Negative aspects

of close relationships and heart disease," *Archives of Internal Medicine* 167, no. 18 (2007): 1951–57.

7. M.J. Rohrbaugh, V. Shoham, A.A. Cleary, J.S. Berman, G.A. Ewy, "Health consequences of partner distress in couples coping with heart failure," *Heart and Lung* 38 (2009): 298–305.

chapter five

CAREGIVING: CAN YOU CARE TOO MUCH?

Caregivers can be people of all ages. However, for now, caregivers are most often members of the baby boomer generation. Demographically, they are simply more likely to be in a position in which they have one or more persons to care for or worry about. While many baby boomers are still working and planning for retirement in an unstable economic climate, combined with an uncertain future life expectancy of their own, they are also increasingly confronted with taking care of a parent, a spouse, or both. Middle-aged adults may also be trying to manage their own health problems in addition to caring for their own nuclear families. Needless to say, the stress of all of this can be overwhelming.

Baby boomers, often considered the most resilient generation in history, are experiencing cracks in their armor. Rates of depression are skyrocketing among baby boomers and middle-aged adults, with men aged forty-five to fifty-four having the highest suicide rate in the country for the second year in a row.[1] Equally as disquieting are rising rates of illicit drug use and binge drinking among baby boomers.[2]

No one can pinpoint exactly why rates of depression and substance abuse in older middle-aged adults are rising, but one possibility is that some middle-aged adults and baby boomers are being asked to fulfill roles that are unduly taxing. Chronic caregiving, in addition to being stressful, may be bad for people's health. As we will see, caretaking can result in a number of physical problems for those who do not manage their stress. Further, serving in multiple caregiving roles can trigger a number of unique stressors that are largely new to the current generation of adults feeling pulled to serve in helping roles.

If you are one of the millions of people taking care of or worried about an aging parent, you know that caretaking concerns do not occur in a vacuum. Because people have begun having children later, some who are taking care of parents are still raising young children of their own. Even when children are relatively old, some parents may still be providing financial help in an increasingly difficult economy.

This chapter will focus on how we can feel pulled into the caretaking role and how the nature of caretaking can take on a life of its own, especially for boomers and those in the "sandwich generation." There are important psychological reasons that this can happen. Understanding the psychological dynamics of caretaking can help us realize the ways we can control situations that before may have made us feel helpless. Additionally, knowing about some of the negative consequences of caretaking too much can remind us of the risks of not taking care of our own body and mind.

Although boomers might be more likely to find

themselves in a caretaking role, all of us, at any age, can suffer from caring too much.

The Magnetic Pull of Caretaking

Caretaking requires an innate ability to multitask, but even for those who are gifted at dividing attention, things get overlooked. Many adults caring for parents or spouses are brilliant in their roles when they are taking care of others; it is their own bodies and minds that are neglected. Consider the case of Suzanne:

Suzanne is a sixty-four-year-old woman who is the primary caretaker for her mother, who lives in a nursing home and has dementia. Although Suzanne has other siblings, since she lives closest to their mother, she assumes the majority of her mother's care. She visits her mother religiously, takes her to all medical appointments, and deals with the staff in her mother's facility whenever there are issues. In addition to taking care of her mother, Suzanne also spends a great deal of time helping her son, who has a number of problems related to substance abuse and unemployment. Though Suzanne is meticulous in managing the details of her mother's life and trying to help out her son, the rest of her life has paid a price. Her husband complains that she is not available, she has gained over thirty pounds in the last year, and she does not exercise, even though she says she would like to. Added to all of that, Suzanne needs to keep working in a stressful job so she and her husband can make ends meet.

Suzanne's life is not unfamiliar to the millions of people who are taking care of parents, children, and maybe even a spouse. With all of these demands, it is not surprising that taking care of oneself falls off of the radar screen. However, not taking care of oneself has a number of negative consequences. People in Suzanne's situation can be more vulnerable to physical illness themselves because of a lack of self-care. Additionally, rates of depression are high in caretakers, and long-term depression also contributes to problems with health. But this information often does little to convince people like Suzanne that self-care is important. Why?

People caught up in the spiral of caring for others often suffer from the belief that taking care of others is more important than caring for oneself. Though some theories in psychology have tended to pathologize people who focus on the needs of others, it is important to remember that when the field of psychology was developed in the beginning of the last century, caretaking of parents was not nearly the concern that it is today. Remember, the lifespan in the 1920s was around fifty-four years of age! Though the need to focus on others so much is historically unprecedented, some people do become overidentified with the caretaking role. Not balancing out the role of caregiver with other important identities has several disadvantages.

For many people, the pull of caring for family members is strong. Not only does caring for one's "tribe" have a biological advantage, in terms of preserving one's family lineage, it is also an important religious and community value that many people hold. That said, we all know people for whom taking care of others seems to become dogmatic or even self-destructive. For people like Suzanne, their focus on others leads them to neglect themselves. The reality is, no matter how much we want to believe that we are excellent caretakers, we can't be as effective at helping others when we don't manage our own physical and psychological health.

Sometimes, the person who ends up being the

caretaker of parents is the one child in the family who may have had a more distant familial relationship. This seems counterintuitive, right? But often it is the adult child who was not as close to their parents growing up who feels a responsibility to help, especially if other siblings seem to lack interest. Motivations in such situations are complicated but can relate to guilt about a stormy adolescence or leaving home early. In other situations, feeling obligated toward caregiving can relate to feelings that grown children did not get everything that they needed from parents or maybe that other siblings got more than they did. This may also seem surprising, but children who do not feel that they got enough from their parents are often eager to try to "give back" at the end of a parent's life. Indeed, taking care of a parent can result in a longed-for last chance to have the kind of relationship that was not granted in childhood. Unfortunately, none of us can get what we did not get before from our parents when they are ill. We cannot redo our childhoods. When we serve as caretakers, sometimes we are giving what we wish we were getting or would have gotten when we were children.

For all of us, emotionally separating from our family is difficult. Setting boundaries with family members is hard, even in the best of circumstances. When we separate from our parents and allow ourselves to live independently from them, there is often a feeling of loss. In the field of psychology, we consider this loss a normal part of adult development. When we allow ourselves to develop meaningful relationships away from our parents we have to give up things from our past, and this involves both sadness and grief. Among what we need to let go of is the security of parental relationships or ideas about what we may have wanted (but did not get) from our parents.

Sometimes letting go of our childhoods feels like it is simply too difficult. Focusing on ourselves, our relationships with our spouses, and on our own careers and life successes can make us feel guilty. It can seem almost as if the task of being a grown-up makes us feel bad that we are not still at home and keeping an eye on our parents.

Of course, this is more difficult in situations in which our parents are conflicted about us growing up and moving on. For example, many people I see who have difficulties feeling confident in their own adult lives are those who were aware that their parents had some investment in their staying young forever. When children move out of their parents' homes, it is a loss for parents too, particularly when parents found a great deal of satisfaction in parenting. Parents have to navigate the terrain of loss and grief as well. When children become adults, parents have to find other interests beyond caring for children.

In my experience, when both parents and children cannot manage the necessary losses required for separation, it can make caretaking for elderly parents much more difficult. People in Suzanne's situation are driven to help, but not in a way that also ensures their own self-care. It is as if the act of caretaking replaces the emotional desire for a different and better relationship with parents. When these dynamics are at the forefront, taking care of others becomes compulsive. Guilt about managing one's own life is overwhelming. People often say that taking care of themselves is selfish and they cannot imagine any role other than caretaking that they might play.

The Physical and Psychological Costs of Caregiving

Though it might sound as if people in Suzanne's situation are not conflicted about their role as a caretaker, this is often not the case. I have seen many people over the years like Suzanne who become quite depressed and anxious about the pull to take care of parents or a spouse. Not all caregivers become depressed and not all caregivers suffer. In fact, as we will see, there may be some advantages to caregiving. However, there is a fair amount of data that caregiving can negatively impact both emotional and physical health. Older adults caring for spouses have higher rates of depression, anxiety, and distress, particularly when caring for spouses at home.[3] Prolonged caregiving, again, often when provided in one's home, has been associated with an increased risk of mortality in caregivers.[4] Reasons for this are not entirely understood. Some researchers speculate that chronic caregiving results in altered immune responses, creating a scenario in which caregivers are more at risk for illness. However, another possible explanation is that only certain caregivers are at risk, particularly those who become depressed while in the role of caregiver. Depression is associated with the development and exacerbation of some illnesses.[5] In particular, depression has been linked with heart disease, the number one cause of death in both men and women in industrialized societies. Anxiety is also thought to be linked with heart attacks in people who already have atherosclerosis.[6] Findings regarding anxiety and the development of illness are less clear, however, and may be due to the fact that depression and anxiety often occur together. Nevertheless, chronic depression and possibly anxiety can have negative health consequences and may explain why caretakers have more health risks.

It is important to avoid using drugs or alcohol to self-medicate and deal with stress. At least one study has found that caregivers who feel burdened by their role are likely to drink more alcohol.[7] Although drinking more may seem to have some short-term benefits, it is not a good way to manage stress. For example, some people drink because it helps them get to sleep. In fact, alcohol can actually disrupt deep sleep, which is thought to be important in terms of supporting our immune systems.

Caretaking may actually have some benefits. Helping others and being altruistic has also been found to result in better health.[8] Additionally, for some caregivers, providing around fourteen hours of care per week to a spouse was associated with a decreased risk of mortality.[9]

The jury is still out regarding how detrimental caretaking is and why. Like all interpretations of medical and psychological research, individual results, not group ones, matter the most. In other words, how we all feel on a day-to-day basis and how we manage stress, no matter what kind it is, should be the determining factor in whether or not we choose to change our behaviors. If loved ones provide care and can avoid depression, severe anxiety, and excessive use of alcohol or drugs, this is likely to be protective against the development of illness. Although it may not feel like it, we all have options in how we manage stress. In caretaking, like in many other things in life, it is often not about what you do but how you do it.

For many, caretaking does not feel like a choice. Most of us would not turn away a spouse or parent if they really needed our help. However, the importance of taking care of yourself too cannot be overstated. The most important thing for caretakers to know is that if you don't take care of yourself, it will be much harder to care for others. But this is easier said than done. One of the main difficulties of the people I see in Suzanne's situation is they don't know how, or don't feel entitled, to ask for help.

Help For Helpers: How to Take Care of You

Getting help when you are a caretaker can be very difficult. People who are particularly identified with being a caretaker may not feel like they can ask for help. Those of us who serve in caretaker roles, either personally or professionally, can suffer from the idea that we are the only ones who can take care of things. Though we might make quiet justifications to ourselves, such as, "There is no one to help me," or "Everyone else is too busy," the difficulty of many caretakers is often related to a less virtuous idea. This idea often goes something like this: "I have to take care of my spouse or parent or friend because no one else can do it as well as I can." This is a hard belief to admit, but trust me, those of us in caretaking roles believe this on some level. It is nothing to be ashamed of. The attitude of being self-sufficient and a good caretaker can lead to a great deal of success in life. However, the belief that you are the only one who can take care of things can also lead to a great deal of strife. People who take care of others too much without respite are often quietly resentful. On the outside, they may appear as if they have it all together and are in control; on the inside, they may be sad, lonely, and angry that they have to hold everything up.

Letting go of this belief is an important step to realizing that others can offer help. Attitude matters a lot. When researchers looked at attitudes and beliefs among caregivers, they found that people who believed that caregiving was an obligation, that it had to be provided by family members, and that individual interests should be set aside to care for a relative, were more prone to depression.[10] These findings make sense. Caregiving can result in loneliness and sadness, especially if you feel that you have to give up your own interests.

But what can you do if you feel that you have no choice? Many people caught in a caregiving role feel helpless. Additionally, the reality of most people's financial situations often limits the kind of outside help that they can afford. Maybe you cannot change the fact that you need to care for the person you love, but there are a number of ways to approach it—beginning with asking for help. Below are some ideas that you may not have considered.

Did you know that Medicare usually provides mental health coverage for your aging family member? Consider asking a professional to see your mom, dad, or other family member coping with illness. Some clinicians and organizations provide home visits or visits to long-term care facilities if the patient is not mobile. The elderly with untreated depression or anxiety have a harder time functioning and being as independent as possible. Psychotherapy for the elderly can improve quality of life.[11] Many caretakers have reported to me that once a family member receives psychotherapy, he or she often seems more independent.

Find support on the Internet. There is a wealth of resources for caretakers online. Check out strengthfor caring.com as well as netofcare.org for comprehensive sources on support for elders, caregivers, and people who want resources on specific illness-related concerns. There is also information on issues of diversity in caregiving. Other helpful sites are www.lotsahelpinghands.com and www.caring.com.

Plan for the future. If you are not yet in a caretaking role but think you could be, think about money. Though many of us are taught that we should not speak about financial matters, it is more important than ever to think about financial issues with family members. Talk with your parents about what they can afford. Be realistic about the future. Do your parents expect you to provide care? If not, how do they plan to take care of themselves? If you are worried about a spouse, talk with him or her about what the two of you can honestly afford if one of you becomes ill. What if one of you had to stop working? Do you have disability insurance and long-term care insurance? If you can afford it, talk to a lawyer who specializes in elder and estate planning.

Perhaps most importantly, have people close to you (as well as yourself) complete advance directives. Advance directives are legal documents that allow people to express what kind of care they want to receive when or if they are too ill to express their wishes. Such decisions include being intubated (receiving a breathing tube), being resuscitated in the event of a cardiac arrest, and so on. Again, although having to think about such things is scary and anxiety provoking, it is difficult and unfair for caretakers to be put into a position of having to make such decisions without having thought it through with those they are caring for.

Having realistic discussions now often prevents being put in a position later on in which you are making all of the decisions while managing both emotional and financial costs.

Finally, don't put pressure on yourself. None of us knew when we were born that life was going to be this long and that many of us would have to worry about our family members in this way. You can have mixed feelings about having to care for a parent or spouse. You also get to decide how actively you want to be involved. There is no right or wrong answer about what to do. What matters most is that you are conscious about what you choose.

Chapter 5
Coping Checklist

- When taking care of someone you love, remember that your life satisfaction is equally as important as the patient's. Optimal caretaking cannot happen if you don't take care of yourself.
- If you think you are the only one who can provide care, challenge this belief. Ask why you might need to hold on to this idea.
- If you have had a difficult relationship with one or both of your parents, know that caretaking at this stage in life will be difficult. You might need additional support or therapy to help you cope with and manage your feelings.
- Remember that no matter what you do for your parent at this stage in life, it will not alter your childhood. Unfortunately, childhood is fixed and we cannot undo it.
- If you find yourself drinking more alcohol or wanting to medicate with other legal or illegal substances, find a therapist or program that can help.
- Find support on the Internet. Utilize the wealth of resources available for caretakers.
- Offering what you can to your family member who is ill is a worthy goal. Feel confident in finding the best care for the patient in your life, but remember that no one can be a perfect caretaker. So when caretakers don't get it right 100 percent of the time, acknowledge the difficulties caretakers face and be thoughtful about decisions regarding who will care for the person you love.

Notes

1. P. Cohen, "Rise of suicides in middle-aged is continuing," *The New York Times*, June 4, 2010.

2. "National Survey on Drug Use and Health," Office of Applied Studies, Substance Abuse and Mental Health Services Administration, December 29, 2009.

3. S.L. Lavela and N. Ather, "Psychological health in older adult spousal caregivers of older adults," *Chronic Illness* 6 (2010): 67–80.

4. P. Reiss-Sherwood, B. Given, and C. Given, "Who cares for the caregiver? Strategies for providing emotional support," *Home Health Care Management and Practice* 14 (2002): 110–21.

5. C.J. Holahan, S.A. Pahl, R.C. Cronkite, C.K. Holahan, R.J. North, and R.H. Moos, "Depression and vulnerability to incident physical illness across 10 years," *Journal of Affective Disorders* 123 (2010): 222–29.

6. N. Frasure-Smith and F. Lesparance, "Depression and anxiety as predictors of 2-year cardiac events in patients with stable coronary artery disease," *Archives of General Psychiatry* 65, no. 1 (2008): 62–71.

7. K. Rospenda, L.M. Minich, L.A. Milner, and J.A. Richman, "Caregiver burden and alcohol use in a community sample," *Journal of Addictive Diseases* 29 (2010): 314–24.

8. S. Post, *Altruism and Health* (New York: Oxford University Press, 2007).

9. S.L. Brown, D.M. Smith, R. Schulz, M.U. Kabeto, P.A. Ubel, M. Poulin, et al., "Caregiving behavior is associated with decreased mortality risk," *Psychological Science* 20, no. 4 (2009): 488–94.

10. A. Losada, M. Márquez-González, B.G. Knight, J. Yanguas, P. Sayegh, and R. Romero-Moreno, "Psychosocial factors and caregivers' distress: Effects of familism and dysfunctional thoughts," *Aging and Mental Health* 14, no. 2 (2010): 193–202.

11. J. Arehart-Treichel, "Psychotherapy changing lives of elderly patients," *Psychiatric News* 36, no. 2 (2001): 12.

GETTING SUPPORT

The idea of getting support when you are dealing with a loved one with a chronic illness sounds simple. Just talk to someone, right? But getting the social support we need in our increasingly fast-paced world is difficult. Given our cultural tendency to deny sickness and death, it is actually hard to find someone to talk with about illness. Many people tell me that they have tried to talk with friends about a parent's or spouse's illness, only to be met with a superficial "That's too bad" and then a polite change of subject. It's crucial not just to find someone who will listen but also to develop the skills you need to talk about illness.

Feeling isolated while dealing with the illness of a loved one can have negative psychological as well as physical implications. This chapter will address the consequences of not getting support and will offer specific tools for finding the right people to talk to, including how to use electronic media and the Internet to decrease feelings of loneliness.

Loved Ones Suffer When Patients Suffer

People who are socially isolated not only feel lonelier, they also are prone to depression, anxiety, and a number of physical problems. Lacking social ties is associated with increased mortality, and having social support is linked with a longer life span.[1] In a landmark review, social isolation was as strong of a risk factor for mortality and the exacerbation of illness as cigarettes, obesity, a sedentary lifestyle, and high blood pressure.[2]

Having both emotional and tactical support is crucial for all people impacted by illness. This is particularly true for spouses who live with someone who is ill and who may be serving in an informal caretaking role. People with ill partners experience more physical symptoms and emotional and spiritual distress and are at increased risk for depression and cardiovascular disease.[3] Measures of heart rate and blood pressure, often referred to as cardiovascular reactivity, are often higher in formal and informal caretakers and are thought to be a cause of heart disease.[4] When loved ones feel isolated, they may not take care of themselves, which can compromise their physical health. Additionally, as relational beings, we are emotionally sensitive to the suffering of others, especially when they are close to us. Researchers have examined the physical effects of simply watching people suffer physically. One study looked at spousal reactions to partners with osteoarthritis.[5] Both the partners with arthritis, as well as strangers, were asked to carry heavy logs, which was demonstrably painful to spousal observers, who watched videos of the activity. Spouses developed increased heart rate and blood pressure when watching and talking about their partners suffering, more so than when watching a stranger engage in the same painful activity. The stress and emotional strain of seeing a loved one suffer really can be hazardous to your health.

It's not only spouses who experience distress when someone they love has a chronic illness. Whatever your role is in dealing with someone who is ill, finding support, especially if you feel distressed, is an important investment in your health. Excessive stress and negative feelings are bad for our bodies.

Fortunately, we have control over how we handle stress. Getting social support is an important buffer against the negative physical and emotional effects of stress. Contact with others who want to help you is just as important as the attention you give to the patient in your life.

It's one thing to realize intellectually that you should have support; it is much harder to get it. Barriers to obtaining social support are real and stem from two main reasons: 1) it can be a challenge to find people who can tolerate hearing about illness enough to engage in empathic listening, and 2) it can feel hard to pull away emotionally or physically from someone who is ill. I will discuss these concerns in the next two sections.

Know What You Want

Many people are uncomfortable and awkward when it comes to discussing illness. Our cultural tendency to deny death and physical vulnerability creates social situations in which people who summon the courage to try to talk about it may be met with a lack of support. Though many of us know when we feel unsupported—such as when people change the subject when we try to talk about something emotionally difficult—it can be harder to know what we want in terms of support and what we reasonably should expect from others.

In order to get support, we often have to assert ourselves. Though some people are fortunate enough to have found friendships that are mutually beneficial, sometimes friendships can be one-sided. Most of us have had friends who use the relationship to talk about their problems, and when the opportunity to listen reciprocally arises, they may fall short. These friends often don't realize that they are not great listeners, and they simply approach friendships by being focused on themselves. When trying to get support, it is important to know from whom you are trying to get it. Make sure you put thought into who you want to talk with. Think of people you know who are good listeners. You may have a friend you care about, but if you think they will not be in a position to listen to what you are going through, pick someone else. It might seem like this is selfish or judgmental; it's not. Think of it this way: you are taking a risk in expressing yourself, so make sure that the risk is a sound one. We can never predict how people will behave, but we can invest in trying to predict who might get it right.

Second, think about what you want to say to someone before you decide to open up. Equally as important, consider what kind of support you would like to receive. We all have different coping strategies; some of us want practical support and advice, others want someone who will listen and let us vent, and some really need people to be emotionally empathic. We may want all of these things. Think about a wish list involving the kind of person who you imagine could meet your emotional needs. Using media figures who listen to others, do you want to talk with a Dr. Phil type of person or someone more like Oprah? In other words, think about what you want and then ask for it. For example, you could say to a friend, "I want to talk about what my family member is going through. I don't need practical advice. I just want to talk about how stressed out I am with someone who can listen to me and realize how hard this is." This might seem overly simplistic, but I have been surprised over the years by the number of people who have not given thought to what they want or even what they mean when they say they want someone to listen. If we don't know what we want from people, it is harder to get our needs met. Realistically, it is our responsibility to think about and articulate what our needs are. People often don't know what we need until we tell them. It is not strange to articulate the kind of support you want or need. It is just a good use of your time. Work on feeling entitled to express your wish for the kind of conversation you want to have.

Many people dealing with ill loved ones, particularly spouses, find it helpful to talk with others in the same situation. One great way to get help from like-minded people is to go to a support group. Finding the right support group can be tricky, however. Groups can involve complicated dynamics, so it is crucial to find a group in which members are compatible. If group members don't get along, just going to meetings can feel stressful. Over time, members of a support group can develop warm feelings for one another and become nurturing friends. In this way, a group can be a great investment.

One other caveat about groups is this: If you go to a group for family members of people who are chronically ill, over time you will hear about how diseases progress. Though some people can tolerate this, others find this overwhelming. For example, I once saw a woman whose husband had brain cancer, and she was eager to go to a support group to talk with others about how they coped. She quickly realized that when she would attend the group, she would hear from others that their family member had become worse or, in one case, died. It had not occurred to her that this would be a part of what she would experience in the group. Hearing about bad news was too overwhelming, and she never attended the group again. I always tell people that if something makes you feel worse, don't do it. Knowing what you might be signing up for helps to avoid unexpected pitfalls later on.

If you can't find a group that you feel comfortable with or if you live in an area where there are no groups, consider starting one of your own. A colleague whose husband developed a degenerative chronic illness wanted to talk with women whose husbands were terminally ill. She started her own group that ended up going on for years.

Perhaps you are not a social person, or maybe you do not have enough time to socialize. In that case, consider reading memoirs of patients and loved ones who have survived illness. Such books offer a number of tips and tricks on dealing with doctors and navigating pragmatic aspects of care. These books can provide needed empathy as you read about others who have lived through similar experiences.

The Internet is another great source of information for people who may not have time for or access to in-person contact. The Internet is full of resources to help you cope as a caregiver. However, be careful with trusting information obtained online when looking up medical information. We've all heard stories about people who were able to diagnose a medical problem by doing online research. However, for every one of those stories, there are countless others about people who became needlessly terrified by a self- or Internet misdiagnosis! But in terms of social support, caregivers and others impacted by illness have created a number of online communities and sources of information.

Beyond the caregiving community, there are other ways that the Internet and social media can help loved ones. One thing that spouses and family members complain about is managing phone calls and emails from concerned friends. Loved ones can feel overwhelmed with the need to provide information and updates when a family member is ill. Though talking with friends can be a source of support, having to manage responsibilities such as returning phone calls and multiple emails can feel draining. You can maximize your time by sending mass emails or using social media such as Facebook and Twitter to post updates easily to a wide group of people at once. You can also create a blog to describe your experiences, as well as those of the patient. You should always strive to communicate in the most efficient way possible.

There is a difference between sharing updates to concerned friends and getting support. You can provide updates and know that you are helping to manage the dissemination of information in a way that you can control. You can also pick one or two people from your social system who you think can and will want to hear about what you are going through. The key here is knowing the difference between those you need to update and those you might want to risk opening up to about how stressed you may feel.

Permission to Take a Break

When someone you love is suffering, illness can seem to be the most prevalent aspect of life. This can be incredibly isolating. I have seen young adults put their romantic and career lives on hold for months or years while bracing for a parent's death, and older adults neglect their marriages while taking care of an aging parent.

Being around others, including people who know what you are going through, is often the only way to remain balanced. Loved ones can be hesitant, though, to take a break from watching patients, believing that they should be available all of the time. Consider the case of Jeff:

Jeff's wife of fourteen years was being treated in the hospital for a rare form of kidney disease. Marilyn's illness required long hospitalizations and extensive treatments that made her tired much of the time. Although Marilyn was completely supportive of Jeff leaving the hospital to go have meals or see friends, Jeff felt that he could not leave, even for half an hour, to go to the cafeteria to get something to eat. When Jeff and I discussed this, he said, "I just can't imagine doing anything that might give me pleasure when she is suffering like this." As I worked with the couple, it was clear that Jeff felt helpless, as any of us would in such a devastating and terrifying situation. On the other hand, Jeff was losing weight, had become very depressed and anxious, and when he was with his wife in the hospital, he was unable to offer her much in the way of emotional support, as his suffering had become overwhelming to both of them.

Getting away is hard. People feel that being around their loved one all of the time gives them control over a situation that is largely uncontrollable. However, never leaving just gives the illusion of control. Some people who can't leave a patient alone are trying to manage extreme anxiety and helplessness through being watchful. In the hospital, such family members may closely monitor a nurse's dispensing of medication, for example. Although it is true that errors of all kinds can occur in hospitals, excessively watching staff and patients can cause problems, and when staff feel overly scrutinized, they can become defensive in a way that can negatively impact patient care.

In Jeff's case, however, he did not stay in the hospital because he was worried about staff. His anxiety was less organized. He simply felt if he left the hospital, something bad could happen. Therefore, he stayed in the hospital in a state of worry and was, ironically, not able to listen to Marilyn when she wanted to talk about how she was feeling about her illness and treatment.

As I got to know Jeff, it also became clear that he felt that if he were to do anything pleasurable, it would feel like a betrayal of Marilyn. It was as if his pleasure would somehow make her suffering worse. Of course that was not true; Jeff was as devoted a spouse as anyone could be. His wife wanted him to leave the hospital, and I noticed that when he did, her mood was better and she felt relieved that Jeff was taking care of himself. Jeff felt what a lot of spouses feel, however. The impact of illness affects couples in a unique way. For many couples in long-term relationships, it can be hard to think about and claim an individual identity when a partner is dealing with a severe illness. In other words, a patient's illness is the couple's illness. However, when loved ones feel as though they have to suffer in the same way as the patient, there can be a confusing merging of identities. Patients need loved ones to be strong. Paradoxically, being strong means that loved ones gather the necessary strength needed for self-care and getting support from others.

Loved ones cannot ever really know what it is that patients go through; they just have to be witnesses to suffering. We may try to understand, listen, and pay attention, but we can't actually know what anyone else is experiencing. This limitation of our understanding can be hard for us. Sometimes loved ones feel that if they do not suffer too, and suffer in just the right way, then they are not being empathic. This is not accurate. Empathy is when we feel for someone else, not believe that we have to become that person. The reality is, we can feel deeply about someone else's suffering and focus on ourselves at the same time.

So how do you tell yourself it is okay to take a break? Remind yourself that getting help for you is as important as getting help for the patient in your life. Partners who don't cope well with illness and who become depressed may be less supportive of patients.[6] Again, you can't emotionally help anyone if you don't take care of yourself. Taking care of yourself, in this context, means getting support.

Taking this first step, especially when it seems that no one could understand, can be scary. Although Jeff was worried that experiencing enjoyment might be a betrayal to his wife, he also felt that engaging in any kind of normal activity was a kind of betrayal to himself and his needs. Jeff was aware on some level that he was neglecting himself as well as his wife, and he felt guilty and anxious about both. He desperately wanted to talk with people about what he was going through, but his experiences with his friends and other family members told him they were not understanding. This was likely true to some extent. Friends and family are sometimes terrified by severe illnesses, especially when they occur in younger adults, and though they might want to be helpful, they often don't know what to say. Platitudes can be common. Who wants to hear well-meaning friends say such unhelpful things as, "Well it could be worse, right?" (Often the answer is, "Not really"), or "Illness is a gift; you can learn a lot from it." (And the answer is, "Maybe, but it's a gift I don't want.") The reality is that many people do not know how to respond when talking with someone affected by illness. So make sure you know what you want and need in a friend or support system, and find the people you need to listen to you.

CHAPTER 6
COPING CHECKLIST

- If you are not used to seeking help or getting social support, develop a wish list in your mind regarding the kind of support you would like to receive. Be specific—people can offer varying kinds of support.
- Don't waste time talking with people you suspect won't understand. Look for people who have been in a similar situation or who communicate the energy to empathize.
- Use the Internet. Create a blog. Develop a mass email list or use social media to provide those you know with updates on the patient's care and progress.
- If communicating with friends and family is too much, delegate this to someone you trust.
- Decline phone conversations if you are feeling overwhelmed. Take calls from people you think will be the best listeners.
- You do not have to be with the person who is ill all of the time. This does not help. Taking care of yourself does.

Notes

1. J.S. House, K.R. Landis, and D. Umberson, "Social relationships and health," *Science* 241 (1988): 540–45; L.F. Berkman and S. Leonard Syme, "Social networks, host resistance, and mortality: A 9-year follow-up of Alameda County residents," *The American Journal of Epidemiology* 109 (1979): 186–204.
2. J.S. House, K.R. Landis, and D. Umberson, "Social relationships and health," *Science* 241, 540–45. (1988)
3. R. Schulz, and P.R. Sherwood, "Physical and mental health effects of family caregiving," *American Journal of Nursing* 108,

no. 9 (2008): 23–27; R. Schulz, K.A. McGinnis, S. Zhang, L.M. Martire, R.S. Hebert, S.R. Beach, et al., "Dementia patient suffering and caregiver depression," *Alzheimer Disease and Associated Disorders* 22 (2008): 170–76.

4. P.P. Vitaliano, J.M. Scanlan, J. Zhang, M.V. Savage, I. Hirsch, and I.C. Siegler, "A path model of chronic stress, the metabolic syndrome and coronary heart disease," *Psychosomatic Medicine* 64 (2002): 418–35.

5. J.K. Monin, R. Schulz, L.M. Martire, R. Jennings, J.H. Lingler, and M.S. Greenberg, "Spouses' cardiovascular reactivity to their partners' suffering," *Journal of Gerontology: Psychological Sciences*, 65B, no. 2 (2010): 195–201.

6. L.M. McLean and J.M. Jones, "A review of distress and its management in couples facing end of life cancer," *Psycho-Oncology* 16, no. 7 (2007): 603–16.

HELPING YOUR LOVED ONE COPE WITH PAIN

Physical pain is one of the least understood perceptions. It is deeply personal and hard to define. Literally, one cannot understand the pain of another. Not knowing how someone feels, however, does not mean that you cannot be supportive. Loved ones play a tremendous role in the experience of pain, and, not surprisingly, good relationships can be a buffer against the hardships caused by chronic pain.

People who experience pain on a daily basis feel angry, helpless, and hopeless. They can act depressed, irritable, and as if they want to be alone. This can be difficult for loved ones who want to help but don't know how. In this chapter, I will explore what people in pain experience and ways you can help, as well as what not to do.

Acute versus Chronic Pain

There are differences regarding the kinds of pain people experience. One main distinction is between acute and chronic pain. Acute pain has a recent onset and is a reaction to a new injury or surgery. In other words, there is actual tissue damage.[1] This type of pain has immediate physical effects, such as an increase in metabolism and gastrointestinal activity. It also increases the "fight or flight" response. The fight or flight response is when we respond to an injury much like the way an animal responds when being attacked or what our early ancestors experienced when threatened by a predator. When in acute pain, we feel afraid and anxious. From a biological perspective, we feel that we need to fight the attacker or run for cover.

However, when it comes to pain, there is no external enemy. The attacker is inside. In this way, pain can be confusing, as the body understands it as a threat, yet the mind knows there is no real danger. For example, a diagnostic test performed by a doctor may cause pain. Intellectually, patients know the doctor is just trying to help. Physically, though, a patient may feel tempted to punch the person hurting them! In addition to creating feelings of anger, the fight or flight response can cause increases in blood pressure, stomach upset, and even shortness of breath, as our breathing becomes shallow. Though we may consciously know that we are not being attacked, our bodies don't know better. This explains what many of us experience when we are in pain; we may feel like lashing out or simply hiding. Our bodies feel attacked, so we think about fighting or fleeing. Pain sets off complicated physical and emotional reactions. We may not always be able to make sense of these reactions, as they often occur outside of our conscious awareness. But our bodies remember how to respond when feeling attacked, even though there is no external threat.

The good thing about acute pain is that it usually

remits. Think of how you felt the last time you had an injury or surgical procedure; it feels horrible for a few days but then gets better.

Chronic pain, in contrast, is pain that does not completely go away. When pain becomes chronic, the acute injury or tissue damage has usually remitted, but the pain persists. Chronic pain never completely disappears, although some days it can feel better than others. For example, using a scale of 1–10, with 10 being the worst pain we could experience and 1 being pain that is minimal, most chronic pain patients describe that a good day is when pain is 2–3 on this scale.

After six months of constant or near-constant discomfort, pain is considered to be chronic. The shift from acute to chronic pain is biologically complex and involves multiple physical processes, including alterations in the immune system and the nature of the stress response.[2] When pain becomes chronic, there are a number of psychological and physical effects, including depression, slowing of metabolism, sleep disturbance, physical deconditioning, and changes in appetite and sexual behavior. Although pain can start out as a symptom, it can become its own disease. Over time, chronic pain can take over and people can have trouble participating in normal activities. Chronic pain, when it interferes with daily activities such as going to work, relating to others, and enjoying oneself, is often referred to as chronic pain syndrome. This title captures the overwhelming nature of chronic pain and the ways it can intrude on and impact the lives of patients. The stress of chronic pain can be an intense and distressing experience for both patients and loved ones. As we will see, the fight or flight reaction experienced in acute pain can also persist when pain becomes chronic, though in a less intense form. Understanding the ways patients might unconsciously revert to behaviors of protection can help loved ones to understand what they are witnessing in someone with daily pain.

The field of medicine has a long and complicated history regarding the sensitive treatment of patients who are in pain. As many people with chronic pain know, some medical clinicians tend to blame or pathologize people in pain. Though this happens less often today, many patients still complain that physicians resist prescribing certain medications for people with chronic pain and are not as sympathetic as they should be. The reasons for this are complicated and are related to both personal and societal reactions to people in pain. One reason some physicians may have trouble dealing with chronic pain has to do with the culture of medicine itself. Medicine is a fast-paced discipline and one in which cures are expected from both patients and the doctors treating them. When pain persists, many doctors, especially surgeons, are simply not prepared to help patients. A typical example of this is when patients see a surgeon for back surgery. The surgeon and patient hope and assume that surgery will take away pain. Sometimes it does. Often it does not. Many patients have described scenarios of surgeons who simply throw up their hands at a third follow-up visit after surgery. A patient may report that he or she is still in pain and a surgeon may say something like, "I don't know what to tell you. The surgery did what it was supposed to do. Go back to your primary care doctor and see what he or she can do." In other words, doctors and especially surgeons have the idea that they can fix people's problems. Chronic pain presents a unique challenge to doctors, who spend years in training with the belief that they can cure disease. Chronic pain simply does not fit well in this model. Patients often bear the brunt of physician frustration.

When pain becomes chronic, patients are charged with a number of options regarding treatment. Medications are one option, but it is a common misconception that medications cure chronic pain; they do not. Most medications for pain dull uncomfortable sensations, but in many cases pain does not completely resolve. So even when people choose to rely on medications, there are a number of behaviors patients can do to help minimize suffering. This can be a blow to some patients who hope that medicine can provide a cure to their disease. Current recommendations regarding the management of chronic pain include exercising; managing weight; doing physical therapy; pacing yourself (meaning not taking on too much when the patient is not in pain); getting adequate, uninterrupted sleep; increasing socializing and pleasurable activities; and engaging in meaningful work. If employment is not possible because of the level of disability, then volunteer work is suggested. Though these recommendations sound straightforward, for some people in pain, they can seem impossible to achieve. Indeed, pain leaves some people feeling so disabled that doing much of anything can feel like too much.

People in chronic pain can feel miserable and complain that no one understands how they feel. To a large extent, they are right; those of us who do not experience pain every day do not know how it feels to wake up with pain, go to bed with pain, and to wake up in the middle of the night with a body that hurts. That being said, chronic pain can be managed. In many cases, people can function quite well with chronic pain. And while it is up to patients to push themselves to cope with pain, there is much that family members and friends can do to help. There are also things that can get in the way of coping, even when loved ones have good intentions.

Problematic Responses to Chronic Pain

People with chronic pain feel that they should do less, especially if a loved one is willing to take over aspects of daily life. But not moving around or taking care of tasks can worsen pain and increase a sense of dependency in the person who is suffering. As loved ones, we want to minimize distress, but sometimes helping too much can hurt. Consider the case of Keisha and her son, Jonathan:

Keisha has chronic pain syndrome following a number of back surgeries for degenerative discs. Her twenty-six-year-old son, Jonathan, lives with Keisha and acts as a caretaker. Keisha reports pain in her lower back and spasms that radiate down her legs. She has complained about physical therapy, saying that it makes her pain worse. She has reverted to a lifestyle of lying on the couch much of the day and watching television, while Jonathan takes care of all household activities—laundry, cooking, and errands. When Keisha came to the hospital for a pain flare-up, her doctor told her that Jonathan was doing too much for her and that she needed chronic pain management to help her do more for herself. Keisha and Jonathan were enraged at this suggestion and felt the doctor was unsympathetic and unsupportive.

Jonathan and Keisha provide a good example of how two people can work together to limit the functioning of someone in chronic pain. Though Jonathan's intentions were to be supportive to his mother, his willingness to take over all of the household tasks and serve in such a pronounced caretaking role actually kept Keisha from functioning as well as she could.

Medical and psychological professionals agree that for most forms of chronic pain, even minimal movement and exercise helps to prevent muscle deconditioning, which ultimately worsens pain. This is why exercise and movement are commonly recommended as a management strategy for pain. However, movement itself can be painful, and patients often feel that if their body hurts, they should stay still. This is one example of a prolonged fight or flight reaction, with the emphasis here on fleeing. The patients feel they have to stay still, which is akin to hiding when feeling attacked. It is important for loved ones to know that taking over and not encouraging a patient to move can unintentionally make pain worse. Behaviorally, when loved ones take over, it also reinforces the idea that the patient is disabled. This can become a cycle. Psychologists who emphasize behavioral conditioning say this cycle can reinforce, or reward, behaviors that are associated with pain. Keep in mind that the term "reward" in this context does not mean that patients want to be in pain or that loved ones want patients to stay in pain. Rather, it refers to ways that we can unintentionally support a system in which patients are less functional than they could be.

A lot of psychological research has examined the influence of helping behaviors for chronic pain patients. One thing that has been studied is something referred to as solicitousness. This is when loved ones respond to a patient who appears to be in pain by becoming overly anxious and offering to help. A common scenario might be a patient struggling while lifting something and a loved one becoming worried and assuming the patient can't do it. Though it is true that people who have pain conditions may need help, these indirect communications and behaviors can become habits that reinforce the idea that the person in pain is helpless. Research has demonstrated that when spouses engage in solicitous behaviors, patients report more pain.[3] An additional study found that solicitousness was associated with greater ratings of pain and increased disability in men. In this same study, women with highly solicitous spouses had a lower tolerance for pain, performed more poorly on tasks that involved walking or lifting, and used medications more frequently.[4]

In the specific context of chronic pain, the meaning of social support has to be modified. Social support is important for health and coping with pain, but the kind of support provided matters a great deal and, as we will see, depends on the overall quality of the relationship. Some people with chronic pain can get caught in a cycle of feeling helpless and then acting helpless. When patient behaviors signaling helplessness get reinforced, it can paradoxically make pain and overall functioning worse. This is why many programs that treat patients with chronic pain encourage them to decrease what they call "pain behaviors." Pain behaviors are those that signal pain, such as facial grimacing, moaning, and so on. The problem with these behaviors is often not that patients are engaging in them to exaggerate pain, but rather, the behaviors send indirect messages to others regarding the need for help. Pain behaviors do not necessarily mean that patients need help. Encourage loved ones dealing with chronic pain to be as independent as possible and notice your desire to step in and take over. Watching someone you care about in pain can make you feel helpless. Channeling your feelings of helplessness and worry by taking over, however, can do more harm than good. Sometimes the best course of action is to step back and wait. Perhaps the patient is okay. Trust that if a patient needs your help, he or she will ask you. Differentiating your emotional suffering from the physical suffering of the person you care about helps them become as independent as possible and reduces the pressure you might feel to take over and help.

The Importance of Positive Relationships

Not surprisingly, the quality of relationships impacts how patients perceive pain. People who report that their romantic relationships are positive experience less pain in illnesses such as cancer as well as in laboratory studies in which people are experiencing acute pain.[5] Emotions, particularly those related to attachments that feel positive or negative, impact the perception of pain. Good emotions are protective. Thinking again about the fight or flight response, imagine how it would feel to be in pain with a partner or loved one with whom you did not feel comfortable. When patients are struggling with feeling attacked by their bodies, they need an environment that reminds them that they are safe. Again, this is not merely psychological—it has to do with the ways our bodies respond to love and attachment. It makes our minds and bodies feel safe.

If a patient cannot feel relaxed with loved ones or if there is a lot of conflict in relationships, this can make pain worse. This is particularly true regarding feelings of rejection. Specifically, social rejection (for example, being broken up with by a romantic partner) causes activity in the same part of the brain as physical pain, as researchers in one pain study put it, "giving new meaning to the idea that rejection hurts."[6] Feeling alone and unsupported can negatively impact illnesses of all kinds and increases perceptions of pain.

When it comes to pain, it is impossible to separate our minds from our bodies. This idea sometimes upsets people who have chronic pain because they worry that they are being accused of making up their pain or, worse, causing their symptoms. This is not true. Our bodies are physiologically impacted by how we feel, particularly about relationships.

Managing Shared Pain

Chronic pain impacts everyone close to a patient. Although the patient is the one with actual physical pain, emotional pain impacts loved ones who are witnesses to suffering. As a loved one, you can help by managing your own feelings about the person who is suffering. Perhaps you feel disappointed that your spouse is not as active as he or she used to be. You may also find that you feel angry with a friend or parent whose personality has changed throughout the course of his or her disease. Anger and disappointment are common responses to people who are in pain and are limited by their illnesses. Loved ones often feel ashamed about negative feelings. This might even explain why some people become overly solicitous and "helpful" with patients; they may be trying to cover up negative feelings. Negative feelings are normal, and it is crucial that these feelings get acknowledged. Depending on the quality of your relationship, it may or may not be useful to discuss these feeling directly. Loved ones need outlets to discuss their thoughts and feelings about their situations. This is especially important when illness and pain are chronic. The longer illness is present in your life, the more difficult it can become.

Find friends you can talk to. Vent your frustration to someone you trust and who won't judge you. If you can talk openly to the patient in your life, try to direct your comments toward the illness or pain. You can talk about how frustrated you are at the illness, not at the patient. This does not mean that you can't or won't feel angry with the patient, particularly if they are lashing out at you. It is not uncommon for people to report that people in pain are irritable. It is reasonable for you to tell a patient that you understand that they are suffering but that when they express their anger at you, it not only hurts you but also makes it harder to be supportive. The most important thing for loved ones is that they find a way to express their feelings. In the context of a good relationship, negative feelings can be expressed more directly. If your relationship has a history of being tense or conflicted, keep in mind that negative feelings might be perceived as an insult. Consider how you want to talk about your feelings by thinking about how safe you feel in general about expressing yourself. Additionally, how safe does the patient feel with you? Do you have a history of being able to talk about difficult feelings without it escalating into something hostile? If so, this is an indication that you can have a more honest discussion about how someone's pain and illness is impacting your life.

Going back to the issue of behaviors, remember that although how we behave is important, ultimately, the context of closeness and underlying dynamics in the relationship matters more when determining what we should say or do. This applies to all close relationships. For example, the quality of marital relationships is an important backdrop in terms of how spouses interpret behaviors. Behaviors among loved ones may be perceived as positive by patients in happy marriages but negative by patients in unhappy marriages.[7] Consider the quality of your relationship. Are there hurts that have not been discussed but need to be? Are you resentful about issues from the past? Are you upset because you feel that your parent or friend or spouse has not been helpful to you and now you feel charged with helping them? Many of us store up feelings when they are not discussed. If possible, think of ways you might try to talk about relationship problems that you have been holding onto. Such problems often pre-date issues of pain and illness and need to be aired. When people get sick, we are often hesitant to think of our own feelings. It can seem selfish to bring up the past. Of course such discussions need to be timed carefully, but it is hard to be genuinely supportive if you are holding onto past injuries. In the case of chronic illness and chronic pain, not discussing our feelings hurts everyone in the long run. For patients with chronic pain, emotional pain can literally become physical pain, so loved ones can help themselves as well as patients when feelings come out in the open.

Loved ones can do a lot to help people with chronic pain. But it is also the responsibility of patients in pain to take charge of their health. When loved ones let go of what can feel like an overwhelming responsibility, then patients are freer to manage and control their experience of pain themselves. Although suffering in close relationships is shared, taking care of yourself and managing your own feelings is not selfish. In fact, taking care of yourself might be the most generous act you can perform.

CHAPTER 7
COPING CHECKLIST

- Helping too much can hurt. Monitor your own emotions and notice when you are offering to help when it may not be needed.
- Find friends to vent to about the struggles of helping someone in pain. If you can, talk directly to the person who is in pain. But try to direct negative feelings toward the illness, not the patient. You can say, "I am so angry at this disease and how it has changed our lives."
- If you find you are holding onto resentments from the past, think of ways you might talk directly about these issues. It is hard to be supportive when you are angry about past hurts.
- Encourage the patient you care about to engage in activities they have participated in before. Go see a movie. Go out for dinner. Try to not let pain limit the one you love.
- Remind the patient about pacing. On a good day, when he or she is not in pain, suggest that he or she not push themselves too much; otherwise they will be in more pain the next day.
- Encourage the person you care about to exercise as much as tolerable. Remind them that movement ultimately lessens chronic pain.
- Remember that you can only do so much to help the patient with pain. Have your own life. Don't feel that suffering has to be shared equally.
- If the patient's doctor does not seem to feel comfortable managing pain or prescribing pain medications,

suggest that the person you care about see a specialized pain doctor. Such doctors are more at ease with chronic pain, commonly prescribe narcotic pain medication, and are easier to communicate with about pain issues.

Notes

1. R.J. Gatchel, *Clinical Essentials of Pain Management*. (Washington, DC: American Psychological Association, 2005).
2. M. Jacobs, personal communication, August 8, 2011.
3. J.K. Kiecolt-Glaser and T.L. Newton, "Marriage and health: His and hers," *Psychological Bulletin* 27, no. 4 (2001): 472–503.
4. R.B. Fillingim, D.M. Doleys, R.R. Edwards, and D. Lowery, "Spousal responses are differentially associated with clinical variables in women and men with chronic pain," *The Clinical Journal of Pain* 19 (2003): 217–24.
5. M.A. Morgan, B.J. Small, K.A. Donovan, J. Overcash, and S. McMillan, "Cancer patients with pain: The spouse/partner relationship and quality of life," *Cancer Nursing* 34, no. 1 (2011): 13–23; N.I. Eisenberger, S.L. Master, T.K. Ingaki, S.E. Taylor, D. Shirinyan, M.D. Lieberman, et al., "Attachment figures activate a safety signal-related neural region and reduce pain experience," *PNAS* 108, no. 28, 11721–26.
6. E. Kross, M.G. Berman, W. Mischel, E.E. Smith, and T.D. Wager, "Social rejection shares somatosensory representations with physical pain," *PNAS* 108, no. 15 (2011): 6270–75.
7. L.M. Martire, R. Schulz, V.S. Helgeson, B.J. Small, and E.M. Saghafi, "Review and meta-analysis of couple oriented interventions for chronic illness," *Annals of Behavioral Medicine* 40 (2010): 325–42.

AVOIDING AVOIDANCE: STAYING CONNECTED, MINDFULLY

Although friends and family might be supportive in the initial phases of an illness, patients often remark that after a few weeks, people go back to their normal lives and leave them on their own. Why does this happen? Especially as friends, it may be hard to keep up with someone we know who has an illness. The temptation to avoid people with illness is complicated, however, and is related to many factors.

We all have busy lives. That said, illness scares many of us. Out of fear, we may feel things irrationally about those who are ill. This chapter will describe some reasons that we avoid people who become sick. Knowing about our temptation to avoid those who are sick is important. When we avoid patients without knowing why, it not only leaves them alone, it also reinforces guilt that we might feel about our temptation to stay away. On the other hand, we may have good reasons to limit the kind of contact we have and to set appropriate boundaries with friends or family who are ill. Such choices should be conscious ones, however.

The decision about how close to be should be based on thoughtful consideration of an anxious or guilty pull to help versus the genuine desire to stay connected or the need to set limits. When irrational ideas lead us toward avoidance, it helps to be aware of what we might be feeling and why. Becoming aware of our feelings about illness and the relationships we have with those who are ill can allow us to stay connected when we really want to. However, awareness can also prevent us from getting involved when it may not be useful.

Religious Ideas and Illness

Religion is an important aspect of many people's lives. Religious and spiritual beliefs can be soothing and even protective regarding health. In fact, for some, religious attendance is found to be associated with decreased mortality.[1] Helpful religious coping strategies involve praying, the experience of a personal relationship with God, and the sense of knowing what will happen after death.[2] Additionally, the social support and social contact gained through attendance of religious services likely helps with dealing with illness.

However, religious beliefs are not always helpful in dealing with illness. In fact, sometimes religion can make things even more difficult. Problematic religious coping ensues when people think that God is punishing them through illness or when they feel that illness is a reflection of an abandonment by God.[3] Patients who view illness as a Godly punishment suffer more in terms of depression and difficulty coping with disease. The unfortunate tendency of some people to stay away from someone who is ill can be rooted in religious beliefs. Consider the Biblical story of Moses and his sister Miriam. Miriam contracted leprosy and was cast out of the community until she recovered. Leprosy was interpreted as the wrath of God.[4] It's not just Biblical tales that suggest that illness is the wrath of God. In some cultures, people believe that divine power is responsible for the development of cancer.[5] If loved ones believe that illness is a form of punishment, it can reinforce the temptation to avoid those who are ill. In other words, when illness is viewed as God's punishment, providing support can be difficult.

Most people with religious views don't blame patients. In fact, most religions provide services and outreach to those who are ill. The Christian, Jewish, and Muslim chaplains I have met throughout my career serve as caring examples of how religion can be used to help patients and family members affected by illness. Overall, religion and spiritual beliefs are helpful for patients and loved ones in the face of illness. However, when we think of illness as the wrath of an angry God or a result of karmic retribution, to name a couple of examples, we may unintentionally be setting ourselves and patients up to be judged or criticized. This just makes everyone involved feel bad.

We all can feel anxious when trying to understand the meaning of illness. If you are religious and find yourself wondering why someone has become ill or if you can't make sense of a desire to stay away, seek out a religious professional who can help. Priests, pastors, rabbis, and other spiritual leaders are accustomed to helping people think about the meaning of illness. Additionally, any well-trained psychologist should have experience working with people around religious and spiritual concerns.

Fears of Illness Contagion

A common fear, and one that is seldom discussed, is the feeling that one has to avoid people with illness because of a belief that illnesses are contagious. Although this might seem irrational, research suggests that otherwise rational people can succumb to this fear. Historically, people have been terrified of infectious and contagious diseases. This fear has been so pronounced, people have complained since the 1900s about the building of medical facilities in their neighborhoods, as if leprosy, tuberculosis, and even cancer could spread from a building in the area or down the block.[6]

Some illnesses are contagious, and throughout human history we have seen populations decimated by illnesses such as plagues. Because of this, fears of contagion may simply be a part of our consciousness. Although fears of infectious disease make sense, we have also seen examples of needless panic and irrationality (such as people wearing masks when they had minimal chance of being exposed) when it comes to more recent illnesses like SARS, or the "bird flu."[7] Another example of an irrational fear of contagion is the panic around the spread of AIDS by using public toilets or drinking from the glass of someone with the disease. We all know that AIDS is not contracted in this way, yet this fear prevails. How do we understand this? Ironically, we live in a world in which people with colds and flu frequently go to work—and these illnesses are, in fact, quite contagious! In actuality, we should all stay home when we have a cold or the flu, but not avoid people with AIDS or cancer.

Illness scares us. In a state of fear, we are all prone to thoughts that we know intellectually are irrational. Avoiding those we love because we are worried it will make us prone to illness does not make sense, but it is a common feeling. When it comes to illness, nervousness about how to maintain control of our bodies can distract us, and sometimes our anxieties about control become the reason we avoid people who are sick. Avoiding people who are ill does not prevent most illnesses. There are precautions we can take, such as not being in an unventilated room with someone with tuberculosis and having protected sex until both partners have received sexually transmitted disease testing from a doctor. However, most illnesses are not contagious during casual contact. Understanding the irrational fears we can experience helps us to know when we are taking care of ourselves in a genuine way versus when we are hoping to elude the ghosts of illness and death that make us feel scared.

Again, many illnesses are not contagious during casual contact. The real contagions are emotions of panic and fear. When we see other people getting anxious about the spread of a disease or even negative world events, we can wonder if we are not being worried enough! For example, in the aftermath of the 2001 terrorist attacks when mail containing anthrax spores was sent to media and government offices, people were afraid to open their mail. Clearly, the general public was not targeted, but we were all in shock, on edge, and disoriented because of the collective trauma that occurred. The panic about the actual attacks became a story about the United States Postal Service. I remember opening my mail thoughtlessly one day during this time and wondering if I was not as anxious as I should be. But I really was not anxious, and it was clear to me that panic about mail was the one way some people felt they could protect themselves from another terrorist attack. It was almost as if worrying about mail made people feel that they could prevent and control another tragic incident from happening. This is one example of how trauma and grief can lead us toward attempts to take control in irrational ways.

It might sound strange, but fears of illness contagion represent a wish. If illnesses such as cancer were contagious, then we could devise ways to protect ourselves. Sadly, we cannot protect ourselves from cancer, heart disease, or other illnesses except by doing the normally recommended behaviors that are thought to help. And even then, many people still develop cancer or have heart attacks, and we don't know why. This is the main reason illness terrifies us. We don't know exactly what causes many illnesses, and we are not sure what we can do to prevent them. Things happen to us that are unpredictable and unexplainable. Understandably, this makes us terribly anxious. In the face of not knowing something, we come up with explanatory hypotheses to help fill in the blanks.

When we view illness as punishment or when we exaggerate fears of contagion, we are attempting to tell ourselves a story that not only makes sense but also allows ourselves to feel as if we have control. The downside of all of this, however, is that we get distracted from the things we are really afraid of: illness and death. In the process, we may avoid friends and family who want our support and whom we want to help.

Existential psychologists have been saying for decades that the major source of human anxiety is the fear of death.[8] Though it might seem that avoiding people with illness is a way to minimize our anxiety about death, it actually makes us lonelier and more anxious. On some level we know that our fears are irrational. That said, there are times when we may consciously choose to avoid people who are ill. These decisions can be grounded in realistic ideas about what we can and cannot offer those who are sick. Indeed, sometimes people who are suffering do not want our help, and it is okay to step aside.

Guilt Does Not Have to Control You

A close friend of mine who was a part of a wide circle of close friends developed a number of serious illnesses. At first no one knew what was wrong with him. Our friend provided limited information, though for the first year or so many of us frequently asked, checked in, and offered our help. Our friend was hesitant to tell us any details. Over time, he became withdrawn and stopped returning phone calls. As a group, we initially strategized ways we could help this man feel more comfortable with his old group, and we engaged in what I now understand to be excessive attempts to try to include him. He did not want to be included anymore. In fact, the more we tried, the more aggressive he became. What I realize now is that as our grief regarding his distancing increased, so did the anger of our friend, who felt the need to cut out everyone close to him.

As anyone who has ever lost a friend knows, the sudden withdrawal of that bond can be quite painful. I actually learned a lot from this experience in terms of how guilt and anxiety lead to behaviors that can be unhelpful. One of our mutual friends hung on for dear life and tried to do whatever she could to try to maintain the relationship, and yet our ill friend continued to treat her with derision. It was as if the harder she tried to engage him, the more aggressive he became. This sometimes happens with illness. A patient can become so angry and resentful about what has happened to him that he feels the need to lash out at people who are close. In such situations, it is often better to back off, as it can become masochistic when we keep trying to force a connection someone may not want.

This is easier said than done. When friends we have known for years cut us off, it can feel personal, even though it is not. When family members act similarly, it can be even harder. Additionally, with family members, it is often not realistic to step out of the picture and wait for things to change. On the other hand, it is usually not useful for anyone to step in and offer help when they may be subject to abusive treatment. Consider the case of Greg:

Greg's stepmother, Judie, was dying of cancer. Greg never had a great relationship with his stepmother and could honestly say he experienced her as quite abusive toward him. His father never stepped in to intervene. When Judie became terminally ill, Greg felt no other option than to help. Greg's father had practical and emotional support from a number of friends and family members. Yet Greg felt it was his duty to help his father, and even though he felt highly conflicted about his role, he missed several weeks of work so he could be at home with his father and stepmother. Even when Judie was dying, she complained about Greg's involvement, reminding him of the ways he had disappointed her. Over time, and after Judie died, Greg resented his commitment. He felt bad about the fact that he had broken up with a promising new girlfriend; at the time, he thought he did not have energy for her. In retrospect, he wondered if the pressure he felt to be helpful was a result of internal feelings about his anger toward Judie. This was curious to him, as what he was aware of at the time was only how guilty he felt. His father did not pressure him to be involved at the end of Judie's life. Greg acknowledged that the pressure to help his dad was his own.

Greg's example illustrates the downside of providing support when a relationship is ambivalent. Guilt can get the best of us. However, sometimes what presents itself as guilt can be a mask for anger. Guilt and anger are often coconspirators that pull us to behave in certain ways. We may feel pressured to step in even when others may not want us to and may not appreciate our efforts. Sometimes stepping in is more about us wanting to rid ourselves of bad feelings. Greg felt worried about all of the angry feelings he had toward Judie and his father, who failed to protect him from abuse. Paradoxically, his anger and guilt about his angry feelings kept him from knowing that he needed to remove himself from a situation in which his help wasn't really valued. Not only was he unable to rid himself of his negative feelings, he developed more unpleasant feelings that needed attention in psychotherapy.

Guilt is a complicated emotion all of us can feel when someone is ill. Try to consider the meaning of your guilt, especially if your feelings seem excessive to you. We avoid people who are ill for rational and irrational reasons. If guilt is pulling you to stay involved, think about what this might mean. It may be due to irrational fears; it may also be due to the need to protect yourself. When dealing with illness and in life in general, it is important to know the difference.

Avoiding Intimacy: Dealing with Sexuality

Sexuality is an important part of intimacy for couples. Illness disrupts many aspects of closeness, but sexuality is often affected for both physical and psychological reasons. As we age, complications related to illness can make sexuality difficult and tricky. Vascular disease, a feature of diabetes and heart disease, is a common cause of sexual dysfunction in men. Additionally, many people report sexual difficulties following treatments for four types of cancers (breast, gynecological, prostate, and rectal/colon).[9] Such difficulties can last for years. In general, any sexual issues should be discussed with a doctor or nurse. Nurses often have a great deal of experience talking with patients about sex. Physical causes of sexual problems should always be ruled out before assuming psychological issues.

Outside of physical limitations in patients who are ill, it can be difficult for some partners to think about physical intimacy with someone whose body has suffered due to illness. Partners can worry about hurting the person they love. Again, when there are physical concerns such as when someone has chronic pain, speak to a doctor about what is safe. In general, sexual activity rarely "breaks" people with medical problems as long as the couple is communicative.

Some partners feel afraid even to raise the issue of sexuality when someone is sick. The tendency to avoid the topic of sexuality with someone who is sick can stem from a fear of appearing selfish or not compassionate. Most patients, however, don't experience a partner's interest in this way. Rather, patients often tell me that they feel unattractive when they have been ill. Knowing that someone continues to be attracted to them is often reassuring. The key is for couples to have honest conversations about what they want the physical aspect of their relationship to be like. Sexuality among couples has no right or wrong answers. Rather, healthy sexuality involves open and honest communication.

The final thing I'd like to mention about sexuality is related to ideas of sex and the elderly. Stigmas regarding elderly sexuality persist, even though data suggests that older adults are still having sex. Starting with the baby boomers, many older people remain sexually active, including 87 percent of married men and 89 percent of married women in the sixty to sixty-four age range. And for those over eighty, 29 percent of men and 25 percent of women still engage in sexual activity.[10] As boomers age, sexuality among older adults and the elderly will likely receive more attention. Already, elder care facilities are aware of the need to deal with the fact that some of their residents are sexually active. For some elders, staying close through sexuality is not a problem. Psychologically, this is a healthy stance to take. However, for some elderly, especially women, sexual taboos exist. I have talked with a number of women over the age of seventy who feel anxious about their interest in sex. The older generation of both women and men has been subject to sexual taboos that are no longer present. However, this does not mean that some older people do not have intense anxiety about engaging in normal sexuality. For example, I once saw a ninety-year-old woman who was anxious about sexuality. Her husband was no longer interested in sex, and she needed reassurance that there was nothing wrong with her for continuing to experience sexual desire.

Sexuality can be stressful to talk about, but it is a needed part of life for many people. Stereotypes about sex and the elderly need to be abated. There is a range of sexual desire and experiences the elderly have. Negative ideas about sex and older people frequently cause unneeded and unwanted shame.

Final Thoughts on Avoidance

Illness makes most of us incredibly anxious. Irrational ideas about the reasons for illness can cause us to avoid people we want to help or comfort. On the other hand, sometimes we are pulled into helping people who would rather we not. And while issues of sexuality do not apply to all loved ones impacted by illness, it's important for patients and partners to communicate and define how close they want to be. Though we avoid thinking about sexuality among those who are older and even elderly, it is important to remember that for most people, sexuality is an important need.

CHAPTER 8
COPING CHECKLIST

- Worries about illnesses being contagious are common, but remember you cannot catch most illnesses through casual contact.
- If you are religious and find yourself wondering why someone has become ill, seek out a religious professional who can help.
- Consider the meaning of guilt feelings when it comes to helping those who are ill, especially if guilt seems excessive.
- Ill people ignite our own anxiety about death and illness. Know that fears and anxiety are normal.
- Sometimes guilt is a mask for anger. If you find yourself feeling excessively guilty, consider that anger may be an underlying cause of your guilt.
- Many people stay away from people who are sick. Just by offering to be around the person you care about, you are providing a lot.
- Talk to your partner about physical intimacy if it is on your mind. Think together about how you want this part of your relationship to be.
- Illness should not mean that sexuality is discounted. Sexuality rarely "breaks" medically ill patients. Ask your doctor or nurse if you have concerns.
- Being older does not mean that sexuality cannot be a part of life. In your own mind, challenge stereotypes regarding sex and the elderly.

Notes

1. T.D. Hill, J.L. Angel, C.G. Ellison, R.J. Angel, "Religious Attendance and Mortality: An 8-Year Follow-Up of Older Mexican Americans," *The Journals of Gerontology* 60B, no. 2 (2005): 102–9.

2. T.M. Greenberg, *The Psychological Impact of Acute and Chronic Illness: A Practical Guide for Primary Care Physicians* (New York, Springer Science, 2007).

3. T.B. Smith, M.E. McCullogh, and J. Poll, "Religiousness and Depression: Evidence for a main effect and the moderating influence of life events," *Psychological Bulletin* 129 (2003): 614–36.

4. Numbers 12:10–15.

5. J.L. Johnson, L.G. Bottorff, L.G. Balneaves, S. Grewal, R. Bhagat, B.A. Hilton, et al., "South Asian women's views on the causes of breast cancer," *Patient Education and Counseling* 37, no. 3 (1999): 243–54; E.J. Perez-Stable, F. Sabogal, R. Otero-Sabogal, R.A. Hiatt, and S.J. McPhee, "Misconceptions about cancer among Latinos and Anglos," *Journal of the American Medical Association* 268 (1992): 3219–23.

6. D. Bernstein, "From pesthouses to AIDS hospices: Neighbors irrational fears of treatment facilities for contagious diseases." *Columbia Human Rights Law Review* 22, no. 1 (Fall 1990): 1–20.

7. G. Pappas, I.J. Kiraze, P. Giannakis, and M.E. Falagas, "Psychosocial consequences of infectious diseases," *Clinical Microbiology and Infection* 15, no. 8 (2009): 743–47.

8. I.D. Yalom, *Existential Psychotherapy* (New York: Basic Books, 1980).

9. C.B. Harrington, J.A. Hansen, M. Moskowitz, B.L. Todd, and M. Feuerstein, "It's Not Over When It's Over: Long-term symptoms in cancer survivors—a systematic review," *International Journal of Psychiatry in Medicine* 40, no. 2 (2010): 163–81.

10. P. Bloom, "Sex in the elderly. Global Action on Aging," 2000. Accessed August 20, 2011, http://www.globalaging.org/health/us/sexelderly.htm.

VICARIOUS TRAUMA AND COMPASSION FATIGUE

Vicarious trauma is a little-known concept outside of literature geared toward mental health professionals and medical clinicians. It describes the trauma experienced through another that can lead to stress and post-traumatic stress disorder (PTSD) that is not dissimilar from what patients experience. Many spouses and loved ones close to illness experience symptoms of vicarious trauma, both during the illness and after a patient passes away.

The concept of compassion fatigue is also frequently applied to professionals working with traumatized populations. Compassion fatigue has been defined in many ways but essentially refers to the exhaustion that affects those who treat or help people who are suffering. A defining feature of compassion fatigue is the inability to develop emotional boundaries when serving in a helping role. Some believe that compassion fatigue can also result in symptoms of post-traumatic stress disorder.

This chapter will address how loved ones can deal

with the trauma of illness. Illness is often traumatic for both patients and loved ones. As we will see, however, this aspect of illness is seldom discussed, even though many patients experience PTSD. PTSD or PTSD symptoms can also impact loved ones, but this is even less described. The emotional distress of illness is something that can impact both loved ones and patients and can last for years, even after an illness has been resolved. Loved ones are especially subject to vicarious trauma and compassion fatigue.

Medical Illness as Trauma

Post-traumatic stress disorder is on our minds lately as it relates to veterans. However, people with medical illnesses develop PTSD too, and this happens more often than you might imagine. The Diagnostic and Statistical Manual of Mental Disorders (DSM IV-TR), one of the main manuals used for identifying psychological disorders, requires the following criteria for PTSD:

> (a) a traumatic event that involves actual or threatened death, or the threat of physical integrity to self or others, and the person's response to that event was intense fear, helplessness, or horror; (b) at least one symptom of re-experiencing of the event, such as intrusive memories, nightmares, a sense of reliving the event, and/or psychological distress when reminded of the event; (c) three or more symptoms of avoidance, such as avoidance of thoughts, feelings, or reminders of the event, inability to recall aspects of the event, withdrawal from others, emotional numbing, a sense of a foreshortened future; and (d) two or more symptoms of increased arousal, such as insomnia, irritability, concentration difficulties, hypervigilance, and exaggerated startle response.[1]

Those of you who have been seriously ill or know someone who has been may recognize some or all of these symptoms. Roughly one-fourth of medical patients with heart disease[2] and cancer[3] meet criteria for PTSD. Some studies suggest that rates of this anxiety disorder are even higher.

As common as PTSD is, it is striking that medical clinicians don't talk about this more with patients. Then again, maybe it is not so surprising. Talking about trauma requires a great deal of sensitivity, time, and vulnerability on the part of physicians. Medical professionals often experience trauma as well, as least the vicarious kind. Having to watch patients suffer over and over again can be overwhelming. People who are continuously exposed to traumatic events need to compartmentalize or cut off thoughts about the experience. Especially for medical workers exposed to highly disturbing and difficult cases, not thinking about what they are witnessing allows them to be detached enough to continue to go to work every day.

Patients also strive to put away thoughts and memories about illnesses that are traumatic or that involved scary experiences. I always suspect that I am treating someone with PTSD when they tell me about a frightening hospital experience without going into detail. They may describe what they went through with the bland tone someone might use to describe a routine trip to the grocery store. Emotion is often absent from discussions of trauma in people who have PTSD—that is, until someone becomes flooded by feelings, and then they cannot shut them off.

This is why avoidance is a key symptom of PTSD. Avoiding talking and thinking about traumatic events helps people function. It keeps them from being overwhelmed. Avoidance carries a price, however. Traumatic events remain cleaved off from identity, and people can feel lonely and misunderstood. Additionally, when people with PTSD work hard to stave off thoughts and memories, it takes a lot of energy. The effort used to keep feelings at bay is not only exhausting; over time, avoiding feelings stops working. This is why people with PTSD can be subject to intense emotions when an event reminds them of what they are trying not to think about. For example, a patient who had a heart attack and almost died found himself enraged when he was in a restaurant that reminded him of where he had his heart attack. At the time, he was genuinely unaware of why he might be feeling so angry. It was not until I made the link for him that understandably, he was distressed and anxious about this memory. His rage was a way his mind let him know that something was wrong. Additionally, avoidance itself can create unpleasant feelings, which is why some people with PTSD can drink too much and find other ways to self-medicate.

People who have experienced the traumatic impact of illness often long for someone to talk with. Even if they seem like they want to avoid talking about what has happened, it is more likely the case that they simply need to feel in control of interactions in which they talk about illness.

People avoid talking about trauma. Patients, loved ones, and even doctors can all be tempted to avoid thinking about the ways illness is traumatic. Indeed, it was not until 1994 that the Diagnostic and Statistical Manual of Mental Disorders included life-threatening illness as a traumatic event for consideration in the diagnosis of PTSD.[4] Illness makes us all feel vulnerable. But avoiding talking about reality only worsens distress, for all involved.

Medical Trauma and Loved Ones: Secondary Trauma

Ideas of vicarious trauma have often been applied to health care and disaster relief workers as well as mental health professionals who work with severely traumatized populations. Other labels capturing facets of vicarious trauma have included secondary post-traumatic stress disorder and compassion fatigue. These terms carry some distinctions in terms of how they are applied to medical professionals who develop symptoms.[5] Though definitions of how helpers are impacted by traumatized populations seem subject to academic disagreements, it is clear that those who witness intense suffering can experience secondary trauma.

These concepts, however, are rarely applied to loved ones. The foremost author on compassion fatigue, Charles Figley, has used the term "family burnout" to describe the impact of caregiving for family members with medical illness.[6] Yet it is not quite clear that the term "burnout" captures what caregivers experience—and describing caretaking as traumatic may not accurately reflect the experience unless caretakers witness their loved one suffer in an intensive care unit or some other kind of intense distress or pain. However, other authors have described how Figley's model of compassion fatigue can be applied to family caregivers in long-term care facilities. An article in the British journal Nursing Older People notes:

> The degree of empathic response, coupled with carers' ability to disengage or distance themselves from the ongoing misery and feel a sense of achievement or satisfaction with their effort to help the sufferer, produce compassion stress. Compassion stress is the compulsive demand for action to relieve the suffering of others. Compassion fatigue is produced by a combination of compassion stress, prolonged

exposure to suffering or an ongoing sense of responsibility for care of the sufferer, traumatic memories and associated reactions such as depression and anxiety.[7]

Compassion fatigue can be applied to caregivers, especially those who become engulfed by their caretaking role.[7] Becoming compulsive about caretaking is likely a way caretakers try to avoid overwhelming feelings of grief, sadness, and loss. Through this lens, some caregivers may suffer from the avoidance symptoms observed in PTSD: they cut off their feelings and become focused on survival—the survival of the person they are caring for and their own survival through the attempt to eliminate difficult feelings. In my experience with caregivers, the caregiving role can become all-consuming when loved ones avoid the realization that the person they are caring for may die. In other words, when caregiving becomes compulsive and all other aspects of life are shut out, this can be an attempt to lessen grief.

Other than this application of compassion fatigue for caregivers, there is little literature that describes what loved ones experience regarding secondary trauma. While there are differences between illness and traumatic illness, the lines between the two can become blurry. By traumatic illness, I am referring to illness that is life-threatening or in which a patient has experienced painful or difficult events related to the illness. Examples of the latter include patients undergoing transplant surgeries, those who have life-threatening cancers, people who have had serious heart attacks, and those who have had other near-death experiences. I have even seen people who become delirious in the hospital due to drug interactions or treatment side effects experience the psychological effects of trauma. Delirium is a very scary situation, as patients can hallucinate and behave aggressively toward staff. Unfortunately, some people remember parts of this experience and can be haunted by the feelings and hallucinations they experienced. I once saw a woman who had hallucinated that she had killed someone in the basement of the hospital during an episode of delirium. These memories of her hallucinations were so vivid and troubling to her that she had many features of PTSD. Hospitalizations can be scary and traumatic for patients. Loved ones, however, are often witnesses to all of the events described above and can be just as impacted as patients.

Even if the patients themselves do not go on to develop PTSD, loved ones have their own experiences of a patient's illness. In such situations, the term "vicarious trauma" seems to be an apt description of how loved ones who witness serious illnesses might be affected. Consider the case of Ellen:

Ellen is a sixty-eight-year-old woman whose husband, Phil, died following complications of diabetes. Though Phil died in the intensive care unit, his many family members reported that he was kept physically comfortable and died peacefully with all of his relatives at this side. However, after his death, Ellen began telling her children that she felt that her husband was suffering needlessly and that doctors did not do enough to take care of him. These fears also manifested in dreams she had in which she pictured Phil suffering and crying out in pain while others stood by, unwilling to help.

Ellen's experience is not uncommon among loved ones who witness illness and death. Ellen felt helpless and overwhelmed. After the death of her husband, she felt very alone as her children and other relatives appeared to move on. Ellen continued to carry the legacy of her husband but did so in a way that expressed her ideas of her own and her husband's suffering. Ellen had also dealt with her husband's long-term illness and his multiple near-death experiences before he actually died. Many of these events were experienced alone and without the support of other family members. Such experiences can be more distressing for the loved ones who have witnessed such suffering and have felt that they could do nothing about it. For example, when patients are in the intensive care unit, they are subject to multiple uncomfortable procedures. Also, they have a life-threatening illness and may not survive. Patients are often humanely sedated in the intensive care unit to ease their suffering. Loved ones, however, do not benefit from such sedation. They keep an emotional record of how the patient is suffering. In this way, they may be subject to more trauma than patients. Their memory for what happens in the hospital is intact. And most loved ones try very hard to be vigilant when patients are suffering; they are the ones who report to doctors and nurses about how a patient is doing when a patient cannot report for himself.

Fortunately, Ellen sought therapy for her concerns about how her husband may have suffered. Given her symptoms, she did meet criteria for post-traumatic stress disorder, since witnessing her husband's suffering rendered her helpless and terrified. The sense of a lack of control in those who watch someone they love suffer through illness causes intense fear. Not only do such traumas make people such as Ellen worry about their own immortality, it forces them to confront the random and unfair aspects of life.

As I spent more time with Ellen, it was clear that she was completely unprepared for her husband's death.

One aspect of avoidance is denial. Some people like Ellen believe, on some level and in earnest, that they will not experience the loss of someone they care about. In this way, denial and avoidance go hand in hand. Avoiding thoughts and feelings serves as a perfect invitation for denial in which reality is simply ignored.

Managing Feeling Overly Responsible

Illnesses can be traumatic for loved ones. Particularly when illness strikes in unexpected ways, loved ones can be caught off guard. I saw this frequently when I worked with adults who had rare blood cancers. They may have presented themselves to a primary care doctor complaining of fatigue and were given routine blood tests. Many patients reported that they had left the doctor's office feeling okay, only to get a call a few hours later when the lab came back with test results indicating that they had to be hospitalized immediately. Similarly, a person who has a heart attack is fine one moment, and then a loved one finds herself calling 911 because her husband has passed out. The suddenness of some illnesses and the way that life, in a mere moment, can be altered forever is a key feature of how illness can be traumatic. Trauma can also be cumulative, and those who deal with patients who hover between living and dying, sometimes for years, bear the brunt of intense anxiety and fear and a sense of responsibility. Loved ones embroiled in such situations not only think that they have no escape from the helplessness they feel, they also are prone to a sense of over-responsibility.

Family and friends who deal with traumatic illnesses can suffer from the misperception that they are overly responsible for the health and well-being of a patient. Feeling supremely liable when someone is sick echoes some of the issues discussed in chapter 5, in that caretaking can take on a life of its own. As caretakers, we might believe that we can offer better support than anyone else. However, the kind of over-responsibility that can occur in people subjected to vicarious trauma has an additional emotional resonance and goes beyond a wish that they are uniquely helpful. People with PTSD symptoms who have been impacted by the illness of someone close to them are not necessarily wedded to the idea that they can offer a special kind of support. Rather, once someone encounters PTSD symptoms, this sense of over-responsibility is more often related to extreme anxiety, fear, and the need for control.

Witnessing the ways that illness can be traumatic for patients results in a unique kind of helplessness. Loved ones can literally do nothing to help during traumatic hospitalizations or when someone is dying. In the face of such helplessness and witnessing someone else's intense suffering, people inflate the sense of control they have. This becomes problematic when loved ones imagine that they influence things that cannot be controlled. For example, several people have told me that they felt that if they left a terminally ill person in the hospital to get some rest, even if it were only for a brief time, their absence would cause the patient to die. Such ideas torture loved ones and reflect the kind of over-responsibility that people can be subject to. These feelings are a way to attempt to gain control in a situation where, in fact, we have none. This is a common strategy when we feel helpless. As children, when we face uncertainties from our parents, we blame ourselves. When we feel out of control, we find ways to be in control, even if this is not rational. This may be the only reasonable developmental strategy when we are young, but it does not serve us when we are adults.

Feeling overly responsible provides a quick fix in terms of giving us a feeling of more control, but it does not work in the long run. We cannot really influence the trajectory of illness in those we care for. However, if we do not manage anxiety, we risk increasing our suffering and possibly the suffering of those we are trying to help. If you notice that you are feeling overly responsible, think of ways to check this feeling. Offer yourself some reality testing. If you feel that leaving a patient will cause something bad to happen, remind yourself that you don't actually possess that kind of control. We all devise strategies to deal with feelings of helplessness, but taking ownership of someone else's suffering does little to help us cope. Step back. Allow yourself to feel sad and scared. Dealing with the reality of feelings goes a long way toward preventing long-term suffering.

How to Protect Yourself

In addition to acknowledging how you feel, it is important to manage vicarious trauma and compassion fatigue by setting boundaries. Limits and boundaries allow loved ones to stay involved without having to experience the same thing as patients. When we love someone, it can be easy to feel the same things they do. In fact, this is the true root of empathic communication. However, when people we love are ill, it is important to avoid empathic merging. Empathy is important, as patients need to know that we understand how much they are suffering. But empathy can go too far. It can make loved ones confused, as their suffering is unique and different from the suffering of patients. When people are overly empathic, they can develop the same kinds of symptoms, such as PTSD, that patients have. And though this is not uncommon in loving relationships, we can do little to help when we feel the same way as patients do. This is why setting boundaries is important. As loved ones, we are the record keepers of the distress of those experiencing traumatic illness. But we are participant-observers, not patients.

The way loved ones can feel helpless is a normal part of what witnesses to suffering experience. Secondary trauma and the development of vicarious PTSD may be unavoidable. However, loved ones help themselves by monitoring the tendency toward avoidance of feelings and keeping an eye on a sense of over-responsibility. Illness and the potential loss of people we care about are traumatic, but by managing and staying aware of our symptoms, we can ultimately gain more control.

Further, illness in those we love can remind us not only of how much we need other people, but also of our own mortality. For some, thoughts of our mortality and vulnerability can be terrifying. Again, this is a normal feeling. Sometimes we identify too much with those who are suffering as a way not to think about the limits of our own bodily integrity. Overidentifying with patients does not help them or us, however. We all have bodies that need to be taken care of. Hopefully, we do what we can to prevent illness. But even thoughtful prevention cannot assure us that we won't suffer like people who are stuck with illness. It is this unpredictability in life and the random aspects of illness and death that can make us all feel terrified. This is why PTSD is so common. If your body works for now, try to appreciate it. Don't feel that you have to take on the suffering of someone you care about.

CHAPTER 9
COPING CHECKLIST

- Know that illness can be traumatic for patients and loved ones. If you are feeling overwhelmed due to an illness, this is not uncommon.
- Try to notice situations in which you are feeling helpless. Such situations can be predictors for PTSD. If you feel helpless, find someone to talk with about how you feel.
- Remember that as loved ones, our role in whether someone lives or dies is limited. Loved ones are not responsible if someone they love suffers or dies.
- If you feel more responsible than you are, offer yourself some reality testing. If you feel that leaving a patient will cause something bad to happen, remind yourself that you don't actually possess that kind of control.
- If symptoms of post-traumatic stress disorder continue (nightmares, intrusive thoughts, inability to manage affairs, sense of overwhelming responsibility), seek the help of a psychologist who can help you cope.

Notes

1. American Psychiatric Association, *Diagnostic and Statistical Manual of Mental Disorders*, rev. 4th ed. (Washington, DC: American Psychiatric Association, 2000).
2. B. Bankeir, J.L. Januzzi, and J.B. Littman, "The high prevalence of multiple psychiatric disorders in stable outpatients with coronary heart disease," *Psychosomatic Medicine* 66, no. 5 (2004): 645–50.
3. M. Kangas, J.L. Henry, and R.A. Bryant, "Predictors of post-traumatic stress disorder following cancer," *Health Psychology* 24, no. 6 (2005): 579–85.

4. American Psychiatric Association, Diagnostic and Statistical Manual of Mental Disorders, 4th ed. (Washington, DC: American Psychiatric Association, 1994).

5. C.T. Beck, "Secondary traumatic stress in nurses: A systematic review," *Archives of Psychiatric Nursing* 25, no. 1 (2011): 1–10.

6. C. Figley, ed., *Compassion Fatigue*. (New York: Brunner/Mazel, 1995).

7. B. Perry, J.E. Dalton, and M. Edwards, "Family caregivers' compassion fatigue in long-term facilities," *Nursing Older People* 22, no. 4 (2010): 26–31.

chapter ten

DEALING WITH LOSS

Grieving is one of the more difficult challenges we all will face as adults. The longer we live the more likely we are to lose parents, friends, and sometimes our partners. These losses can seem unbearable.

Grieving is not just related to death, however. Throughout our adult lives we face multiple losses. These losses include dealing with illness or even the limitations of aging. Our bodies change as we get older, and we all need to manage the blows that accompany this transition: We may not be able to exercise as efficiently; we gain weight faster and lose weight slower, our eyes and ears don't work as well, and our bodies start to hurt more. More important, however, aging reminds us that we won't live forever. This becomes more apparent as we approach middle age and beyond.

Though we have our own experiences with aging and associated losses, there is also a lot of grieving that needs to take place when illness affects those whom we care about. When people we love get sick, sometimes life is never the same. Illness strains friendships and taxes partners and adult children. People who are ill may distance themselves. Sometimes they do not take care of their bodies, increasing our worry that they might become more ill. When parents become ill, we are reminded of the ways we cannot redo our childhood; this can mean we need to accept that we may not have gotten all that we wanted as children. Illness often involves loss, even if loss does not mean death. Of course, illness sometimes does result in loved ones being taken from us. Unfortunately, death is a part of life, and grieving those we have lost is a part of what many of us will experience.

This chapter will discuss facets of grieving. Though there are many societal expectations about what is normal or not, grieving can take many forms, and there is no right or wrong way to grieve. That said, grief and loss bring up difficult feelings, which are better managed when they are attended to. Ignoring difficult feelings makes it harder to control them.

What Is Grieving?

"Grieving" is a familiar term to mental health professionals. Given my experience with patients, however, I think it is a mistake to assume that this term makes sense to everyone. The concept of grieving, at least as psychologists understand it, is not well understood. In our fast-paced world in which we are frequently kept moving and distracted, we can avoid absorbing loss.

People react to loss in different ways. One mistake, as I see it, in the medical and psychological literature is that there is an assumption that we all grieve the same way. Further, there is also a disquieting trend to label grief reactions as normal or abnormal.

As a point of departure, grief involves sadness and other feelings (that may or may not be overwhelming) related to the loss of something. These losses can be varied and can include the loss of someone through death or the ending of a relationship. However, there are other kinds of losses that affect us: the realization of the limitations of someone we care about who is ill, and the loss of how we can relate to or socialize with people who are ill, for example. We can even grieve losses related to our own bodily limitations as we age. Many athletes have told me that there is often a grieving process associated with the awareness that they cannot perform like they used to.

There are two categories of grief I want to highlight. The first is how to deal with grief when someone we care about dies. The second is the kind of grief loved ones feel when they are impacted by someone's illness. Sometimes, when living with a chronic illness, loved ones need to accept relational losses that are caused by another's illness. At other times, when someone has a disease that will likely end their life, loved ones engage in what is called anticipatory grieving. It is important to note that while I am going to talk about grief and grieving and what some people experience, many in the fields of medicine and psychology have articulated how people should grieve. This is not a stance I wish to take. As we will see, there are a number of problems with prescribed methods and so-called stages of grieving. The main problem with this literature is that grieving is as individual as relationships. In other words, there is no right or wrong way to grieve.

Grieving Death

Regarding the death of someone close, some professionals tend to categorize grief into two categories:

so-called normal grief and pathological grief. These categories have often confused me.

As far as the distinctions of grief go, I am wary of descriptions of pathological grief or even descriptions of so-called normal grief. In almost twenty years, I have seen people react to loss in a variety of ways. Seeing people who have lost their partners after decades-long marriages has made me hesitant to diagnose people who are bereaved. I have seen many men and women reporting good relationships who have lost their partner in the fourth, fifth, or even sixth decade of their marriages. Such a loss cannot be comprehended by those who do not have close marriages or who do not have marriages that have lasted this long. I remember one man telling me after his wife of nearly sixty years died, "Everything we did, we did together. What am I supposed to do now? We talked about it—death—we did. But we never really knew how each of us would manage." This man did go on to develop symptoms consistent with depression, but I found myself thinking, "Who am I to judge his response? This hardly seems abnormal, given the context." Especially at the time, I was relatively young and felt ill-prepared to pronounce his condition, as we often do when we diagnose people. But even now, I find myself critical of models of grieving that are so prevalent in the fields of medicine and psychology. Contrastingly, I have seen people in long marriages seemingly move on quite well after losing a spouse. Some people might look for another partner right away and some never think of being with a partner again. Either way, as long as people are comfortable with how they do things, I am reluctant to make a determination. Relationships are unique. We can never really know what two people mean to one another. When we diagnose grieving, we assume some special knowledge about a relationship that we have had no part of. Though diagnosing actual mental illness can provide a benefit to patients, I am dubious about the role of those of us in psychology and medicine who feel a need to label and categorize grief.

I am not alone in this thinking. Other authors have criticized North American models of grief that include the assumptions that 1) grief follows a specific pattern, 2) the experience of grief is finite, 3) grief occurs in stages, 4) prolonged grief is abnormal, and 5) the "working through" of the grief process is necessary.[1] The authors Breen and O'Connor point out that the way some have framed "normal" grief reactions sets patients up for being pathologized; when patients show too much emotion or, contrastingly, not enough, they are perceived to be grieving in the "wrong way." Indeed, there is a curious tendency to evaluate where someone is in the grief process. However, what could be determined as dysfunctional may be simply a response to extreme or unfavorable circumstances.[2] Though it is true that some people who are grieving become depressed or develop symptoms of post-traumatic stress disorder (PTSD), I see this as a consequence of what patients deal with when they see their loved ones suffer from illness. Loved ones who witness the suffering of patients also suffer themselves. Often they bear witness to this suffering by having symptoms of PTSD themselves, as discussed in the previous chapter. However, in my view, secondary trauma is not the same as grieving.

An article by Megan O'Rourke in a 2010 issue of *The New Yorker* talks about a "one size fits all" model for grief.[3] O'Rourke points out the inherent problems in stage models of grief. People fluctuate in their feelings about loss—sometimes they feel okay and sometimes they do not. Some people can be remarkably resilient about grief. Some people simply do not need to grieve intensely, even if someone they love has died. That being said, O'Rourke points out an interesting paradox: in countries with fewer mourning rituals, people who are grieving report higher levels of physical symptoms (often a marker of grief) in the aftermath of a death.

In other cultures, there are more rituals around grief. In the United States, certain religions have expectations around grief (funerals, sitting shivah, and so on), but our culture as a whole has a curious idea about grief: it should last about a year, and people should move on after that. But what if loved ones can't or don't feel like "moving on"? And what does moving on even mean? Does moving on mean looking for a new partner a year after someone has died? What if someone does not wait a year? What if they never want to find a new partner? As a therapist, I don't think it is unreasonable to ask questions in an effort to help people clarify and understand what is useful for them. But we all have to be careful in asking these questions if we have some idea about what the right answer is. Since grieving involves relationships, actual feelings of grief may be related to how a relationship was valued and understood. If a relationship was close, grieving might be more intense. If not, then grieving might be less intense. On the other hand, even people in close relationships may not necessarily grieve intensely. People have all kinds of different strategies for managing emotions. My point here is that individuals, as well as relationships, are complex and unique. Grieving is similar. Ideas about what is normal should not be imposed.

In perhaps one of the more poignant chronicles of grieving, *The Year of Magical Thinking*, Joan Dideon describes how she waited for her husband to come home after his fatal heart attack by leaving his clothes and shoes for him in case he were to return.[4] She knew intellectually that such behaviors were not going to bring him back, but she held out hope, just in case. Such feelings are entirely common, and as Dideon beautifully articulates, can seem like the only way to deal with a traumatic and devastating loss. For some, the loss of someone they love and with whom they have spent their lives requires them to deal with a new kind of life, and one that they are not prepared for.

Dideon's description of magical thinking is related to worries people sometimes have about dreams or visions of those who have passed away. These experiences are not uncommon and do not necessarily reflect a disturbance in those who are bereaved.[5] It is not unusual for me to hear from patients who are grieving that they have had experiences in which they feel as though those they have lost are still with them. This might occur in a dream, a sense of the presence of the person when my patients are falling asleep, or even a feeling that they may see or sense the person when they are awake. On the other hand, I have worked with people who have had none of these experiences and barely talk about how much the person they have lost is missed. Grieving is complicated, and we all have different ways of handling it. If you are reading this book and have lost someone you love, know that while your grieving can share some similarities with others', it is also a unique experience. There is no one size that fits all. What matters most is how you feel and what you intend to make of the rest of your life. For some, spiritual and religious beliefs can offer a great deal of solace and support. For others, religion and spirituality is not as useful, even when people have spent their childhoods and adult lives engaging in religious activities. How people react toward their religion when someone dies is, again, very individual. Some people experience a renewed call toward religion when someone dies, while others remove themselves.

For example, one very religious man felt the need to avoid religion after his wife died. Though he did not denounce his religion, it took him a couple of years to return to his synagogue. After his wife died, he felt confused as to how his religion could be comforting. He avoided attempts from his rabbi to discuss his feelings and at the time felt that his rabbi was being intrusive. Over time, however, he understood that his desire to shy away from his religion had little to do with his faith. It had more to do with the fact that he did not want to talk about his wife's death. Many people from his synagogue wanted to ask how he was feeling. In his case, being around his religious friends simply made him feel more aware of his emotions. He needed to avoid friends for a while until he was able to understand the meaning of this avoidance in therapy. Once he was able to develop some sense of his emotions, he was eager to reengage in his spiritual and religious beliefs. He also understood how much he had missed his religious community.

The point of this story is that for some loved ones, dealing with illness and grief can be overwhelming. It can be problematic to assume that all people seek solace in the same way. Since I had the privilege of seeing this man in therapy, I could see that he was, in fact, dealing with his grief. He was quite aware of his feelings and was articulate about them. Rather, he simply needed to control how and when he talked about his feelings, and that was largely why he avoided all of his friends, not just those who were part of his religious community. This controlled avoidance was how he kept himself from feeling overwhelmed. Unlike avoidance in post-traumatic stress disorder, however, he was not shunting off his feelings and was using therapy to deal with them. It simply took him time to be able to deal with his feelings around others. The needs of loved ones vary and shift over time. We need to respect what people's needs are at a given moment. People seek support when they are ready. Not judging loved ones in circumstances that no one else can understand is extremely important.

Grieving Other Losses

A patient in his late sixties, while still a very successful professional in his field, realized that he was quite distressed that he had not accomplished more in life. At this point in his life and career, given his age, he knew that there was only so much more he could achieve. Over the course of therapy, he understood that some of his feelings and behaviors had an impact on things not turning out the way he had wanted them to. Specifically, he thought that feelings of envy toward others and the ways that he resented needing them (as success involves some level of relying on others) made it hard to achieve certain kinds of accomplishments. He said to me, "So what am I supposed to do: realize that my life is what it is, deal with the feelings, and try to do things differently from here on out?" My answer was simply, "Yes." This is an ideal example of someone who could come to terms with grieving losses unrelated to death. In this man's case, his grieving did not even pertain to illness or the loss of others (though he did lose more than his fair share of people close to him). He was simply facing what a lot of us deal with as we age: we become aware that life is finite and that some of our best successes may be behind us. I don't want to overstate this, however, as many people can become very accomplished late in life. But there is some truth in the acknowledgment that when a large part of life has passed, there are limitations not only to what we can continue to achieve, but also to how much time we actually have left. This is one of the hallmarks of middle age and why it has been the subject of so much speculation. Whether or not someone actually goes through a midlife crisis remains debatable, but this stage in life is important because many people do suddenly become aware of the finite nature of life.

We all have losses to absorb as we get older. Sometimes these losses are related to aging; sometimes they are simply related to our realization that if we could do some things over again, we would handle things much differently. I remember the year that the phrase, "Youth is wasted on the young" finally made sense to me. I understood that with age comes wisdom, understanding, and perhaps most important, a lack of impulsivity. People who are older tend to think more about things, sometimes have a larger awareness of their feelings, and are secure enough in themselves that they do not act rashly or with aggression when they are disappointed. Once we do enough living, we have been through many situations before. Therefore, we can take our time, figuring out how best to respond, while considering the nuances of our feelings as well as the feelings of others. I do think that grieving becomes easier as we age. We realize that there are limits to how important we are and simultaneously appreciate how much we can hurt people. Additionally, one of the great things about aging is that we often realize that so much of what happens in human interactions has to do with the dynamics of others, even though when we get together with people to connect, we may create unique scenarios that sometimes work out well. At other times the combinations we can establish can become toxic. And in reality, often no one is to blame. To me this is the true definition of grieving. Sometimes relationships work out and sometimes they don't. Illness is one of many factors that can change us and those we care about. In my mind, true grieving is knowing there is so much we can't control.

Loss and Illness

Illness changes life and relationships. Throughout this book, I have tried to describe many aspects of loss and the feeling of helplessness that often accompanies illness. Though helplessness is a feeling that most of us would prefer to avoid, it is a part of life in the same way that illness and death are. While many feelings related to illness are painful, like all difficult feelings, when we can express them with people we trust, we feel safer with the emotional ghosts that haunt us. Additionally, being more aware of feelings and giving ourselves permission to feel them helps us to gain more control of our actions. It also allows us to be optimally helpful to those we love when they are ill.

The survivors and witnesses of those who have been ill do well when they can find a way to absorb loss.

Acknowledging loss is a better term than grieving, as grieving often connotes a formula and prescription about what is right and what is wrong. We all deal with loss differently. A colleague of mine who lost her husband as a result of a rare illness when they were both middle-aged serves as a poignant reminder of how loss can be handled with success. This colleague wrote papers and gave talks about how devastating the loss was to her but has seemed to embrace life in a vibrant way. She has thought about dating, though not a day goes by that she does not think about her late husband. She feels that she can honor his memory by taking care of her grandchildren, looking after her children, and offering as much as she can to her work. She is not depressed but is realistically sad about what she has lost. But she has the courage to go on in spite of this loss and sees the value in giving to others.

The story of my colleague and friend captures the true meaning of this book. Illness and death among those we love seem unfair and random. But they are also sad facts of life. We all get old and we all die. Some of us die early. Those of us who are left behind must manage our lives, but we can do so by honoring those we have lost.

Throughout this book, I have talked a lot about suffering. If someone we love is lost to illness, then we are left to incorporate their identities and memories as we continue on with our lives. The main challenge for all of us in the twenty-first century is that we all have ambiguous futures. We may live a long time and be relatively healthy. We may not. And if we live a long life, we will all encounter friends and family who are chronically ill or lose them along the way. None of us has the answer as to what will be our fate. But by remembering what others have gone through regarding illness, we can acknowledge those who have gone before us and try to prepare ourselves for the uncertain future that lies ahead. The good and the bad news about a long life is that illness will be something that most of us confront. All we can do is be emotionally prepared to help those we care about.

Chapter 10
Coping Checklist

- Grief has no timeline. Ignore the social idea of a twelve-month grieving process. Missing someone you love can last a lifetime. If feelings of hopelessness, helplessness, or suicide persist, consider seeking a therapist who can help provide additional support.
- There is no right or wrong way to grieve. Don't feel pressured to be distressed. Don't feel pressured not to be. How you deal with your feelings regarding loss is up to you.
- Find people you want to be around who can hear about your feelings. If you don't want to talk about loss or feelings of grief, make that clear to friends and people who want to support you.
- Think of grieving as involving how you absorb loss. We all do this differently.
- One "loss" we all have to deal with is the knowledge that life is finite but can be very extended. This can be stressful and taxing. We all will likely confront our own illnesses as we age, in addition to those of people we care about.

Notes

1. L.J. Breen, and M. O'Connor, "The fundamental paradox in the grief literature: A critical reflection," *Omega* 55, no. 3 (2007): 199–218.
2. C.M. Parkes and R.S. Weiss, *Recovery from Bereavement* (New York: Basic Books, 1983).
3. M. O'Rourke, "Good Grief," *The New Yorker*, February 1, 2010.
4. J. Dideon, *The Year of Magical Thinking* (New York: Random House, 2005).

5. L.M. Daggett, "Continued encounters: The experience of after-death communication," *Journal of Holistic Nursing* 23, no. 2 (2005): 191–207.

Photo by Suzanne Sizer Photography

ABOUT THE AUTHOR

Dr. Tamara McClintock Greenberg is a published author and speaker. She contributes to websites like *The Huffington Post* and *Psychology Today* and is an Associate Clinical Professor of Psychiatry at the University of California, San Francisco. Dr. Greenberg provided consultation-liaison services within the UCSF hospitals and in long-term care facilities for over ten years. She currently has a private practice in San Francisco, CA.

CPSIA information can be obtained
at www.ICGtesting.com
Printed in the USA
LVHW022150230120
644554LV00006B/158

9 781599 559391